P9-DXH-842

D0037900

DISCARD

John Forster

Twayne's English Authors Series

Herbert Sussman, Editor

Northeastern University

TEAS 379

JOHN FORSTER
(1812–1876)
Photograph courtesy of the Dickens House

John Forster

By John J. Fenstermaker

Florida State University

Twayne Publishers • *Boston*

John Forster

John J. Fenstermaker

Copyright © 1984 by G. K. Hall & Company
All Rights Reserved
Published by Twayne Publishers
A Division of G. K. Hall & Company
70 Lincoln Street
Boston, Massachusetts 02111

Book Production by Marne B. Sultz
Book Design by Barbara Anderson

Printed on permanent/durable acid-free
paper and bound in the United States of
America.

Library of Congress Cataloging in Publication Data

Fenstermaker, John J.
   John Forster.

      (Twayne's English authors series; TEAS 379)
   Bibliography: p.
   Includes index.
   1. Forster, John, 1812–1876.
2. Critics—England—Biography.
3. Literary historians—England—Biography.
4. Biographers—England—Biography.
I. Title.   II. Series.
PR29.F67F46 1984   820'.9 [B]   84–3781
ISBN 0–8057–6865–3

Contents

About the Author

John J. Fenstermaker is Chairman of the English Department at the Florida State University. His publications include articles on Dryden, Dickens, Emerson, Fitzgerald, and Hemingway and on literary research, composition, and rhetoric. He is the author of *Charles Dickens 1940–1975: An Analytical Subject Index to Periodical Criticism of the Novels and Christmas Books* (1979), and he revised for the Third Edition Richard D. Altick's *The Art of Literary Research* (1981).

Preface

As critic, editor, historian, and biographer, John Forster was an ubiquitous and inordinately powerful presence in the literary world of early- and mid-Victorian England. He formed close friendships with and often exerted significant influence over many contemporary English writers, including William Harrison Ainsworth, Robert Browning, Edward Bulwer, Thomas Carlyle, Charles Dickens, Leigh Hunt, Sheridan Knowles, Charles Lamb, Walter Savage Landor, William Charles Macready, and William Makepeace Thackeray. His name occurs more often than any other in Macready's diaries. Bulwer, who said that "there is no safer adviser about literary work, especially poetry, no more refined critic" than Forster, described himself as "greatly indebted to his counsels" and claimed that "Tennyson and Browning owed him much in their literary careers."[1] Indeed, Browning gave him the manuscript of *Paracelsus* and dedicated the first collected edition of his works to Forster. Bulwer, Carlyle, Dickens, and Landor named him literary executor; he served Dickens and Landor as official biographer.

Forster was "perhaps the one most influential critic of the metropolitan press"[2] during the 1830s and 1840s; he was chief literary and drama critic of the *Examiner* for more than twenty years, serving also as subeditor and, from 1847–1856, as editor. In addition, he contributed essays to most major British periodicals and was editor or business manager of the *New Monthly Magazine,* the *Foreign Quarterly Review* and the *Daily News.* Further, in his time Forster was considered one of the foremost authorities on the history of the Commonwealth period of the seventeenth century. Between 1836 and 1864 he published numerous studies of this era, the best known of which were his five volumes of "Lives of Eminent British Statesmen" in Dionysius Lardner's *Cabinet Cyclopaedia* (1836–1839) and, at the end of his career, the two-volume biography *Sir John Eliot* (1864). His greatest achievements, however, were his literary biographies of Goldsmith (1848) and Dickens (1872–1874); the three-volume *The Life of Charles Dickens* is one of the finest English biographies written in the nineteenth century.

Despite Forster's obvious centrality in English letters during the Victorian age, for more than one hundred years after his death only two minor book-length studies of his life were published: a brief memoir by a friend (1903) and a largely appreciative biography by the nephew of Forster's wife (1912). Some valuable discussion of his work remains generally inaccessible in unpublished dissertations; particularly useful for this volume has been such work by Sister Mary Callista Carr and Elizabeth Johnston. Until most recently, however, the several fine articles by James A. Davies have been the only substantial published scholarship to examine Forster's own writings or to explore his influence on important contemporaries, except for the work done by Dickens scholars interested in Forster's relationship with the novelist. Davies's work on Forster has now reached fruition in his *John Forster: A Literary Life* (Leicester: Leicester University Press, 1983), which appeared just as the present study went to press.

The purpose of this volume is to assist in and to encourage further the process of reclaiming Forster's reputation. Chapter 1 considers the breadth of his literary endeavors and friendships. The remaining chapters examine his own writing as a critic, historian, and literary biographer, assess his contemporary importance, and argue the right to greater prominence in modern scholarship for this eminent man of letters.

I would like to acknowledge my considerable debt to the following persons for their help with this study: to my colleague C. Eugene Tanzy for his advice throughout the manuscript; to my editor Herbert L. Sussman for his patience and encouragement in addition to his valuable suggestions; to the staff of the Interlibrary Loan division of the Robert Manning Strozier Library at Florida State University for their courtesy, promptness, and thoroughness; to Kate Hodges Adams and Steve Lamar Adams for their assistance in collecting materials.

John J. Fenstermaker

Florida State University

Chronology

1856   Retires from editorship of the *Examiner* and gives up virtually all newspaper journalism; publishes "The Civil Wars and Oliver Cromwell" in *Edinburgh Review;* marries Eliza Ann Colburn.

1858   *Historical and Biographical Essays,* 2 vols.

1860   *Arrest of the Five Members by Charles the First; Debates on the Grand Remonstrance, November and December, 1641.*

1861   Becomes Commissioner of Lunacy.

1864   *The Life of Sir John Eliot,* 2 vols.

1869   *Walter Savage Landor: A Biography,* 2 vols.

1872–1874   *The Life of Charles Dickens,* 3 vols.

1875   *The Life of Jonathan Swift* (only Volume I of projected three volumes completed).

1876   John Forster dies February 1.

Chapter One
Eminent Victorian
Character and Personality

John Forster, critic, historian, biographer, merits a place of distinction in the history of nineteenth-century British literature; indeed, he was without peer among British critics of contemporary literature and drama between 1834 and 1856, the years that saw the development of Victorian literature. Yet, even after detailed examination of the dates, places, personal relationships, and writings of this man, his character and personality could remain elusive, only partially grasped. For this reason a short preamble to the biographical sketch seems appropriate.

Who was John Forster? He was most certainly a man of his age, a "Victorian" who embodied, as much as he forged, the tastes, morals, and mores of mid-nineteenth-century England. In addition, his was a success story. Arriving in London at age sixteen in 1828, without friends or introductions but with ambition, some education, a formidable capacity for work, and substantial confidence in himself, he had so mastered literary London by his twenty-eighth birthday that he knew well and in many instances was on intimate terms with the following: actors—Charles Kean, Sheridan Knowles, William Charles Macready; publishers, editors, and critics—Richard Bentley, Laman Blanchard, Edward Chapman, Henry Colburn, Albany Fonblanque, W. J. Fox, Samuel Carter Hall, William Hall, Theodore Hook, R. H. Horne, Douglas Jerrold, John Macrone, William Maginn, Edward Moxon; artists and illustrators—George Cattermole, George Cruikshank, John Leech, Daniel Maclise, Clarkson Stanfield; authors—Lady Blessington, Robert Browning, Edward Bulwer, Thomas Carlyle, Charles Dickens, Leigh Hunt, Walter Savage Landor, Bryan Proctor, Thomas Noon Talfourd, Alfred Tennyson, William Makepeace Thackeray. The list, long as it is, is merely suggestive.

But who was John Forster? What was he like? Certain of his favorite catch words come to mind: "Prodigious," "In*tol*-er-able,"

"Monstrous," "Incredible."[1] He was a huge man who lived a life overflowing with expletives and superlatives. R. C. Lehmann described Forster as a "very big, square, beetle-browed, black-haired piece of solid humanity, with a voice that made the glasses jingle on the table. Yet he would roast you (on paper) as gently as any . . . dove, for with all his arbitrariness and resolute roughness he had one of the kindest hearts that ever beat in the breast of a literary dictator."[2] His young protégé, Percy Fitzgerald, among others, thought of the great Dr. Johnson as an appropriate comparison: "If anyone desired to know what Dr. Johnson was like, he could have found him in Forster. There was the same social intolerance; the same 'dispersion of humbug'; the same loud voice, attuned to a mellifluous softness on occasion, especially with ladies or persons of rank; the love of 'talk' in which he assumed the lead—and kept it too; and the contemptuous scorn of what he did not approve."[3]

His authoritarian manner caused frequent flare-ups with friends, of course, many of whom had notable egos of their own; the actor William Charles Macready's diaries record frequent occasions, often at dinner, when he or Robert Browning or Edward Bulwer was infuriated by Forster's inflexible pronouncements; Thackeray notes in a letter that at a dinner in 1839 Forster did not, surprisingly, say "a single rude thing";[4] on the other hand, at a dinner at Dickens's in 1840, Mrs. Dickens left the table in tears after a set-to between the novelist and his friend.[5]

Such ruptures usually healed quickly, however, and Forster enjoyed friendships spanning decades with each of these literary giants and with others: he was, in fact, Macready's best friend; Thackeray, who was to know Forster's kindness during a serious illness, conceded after a period of public disputes that their differences were not personal but philosophical; Browning dedicated to Forster his collected edition of 1863 and sent him the manuscript of *Paracelsus* inscribed to "my early Understander"; Landor, Dickens, Carlyle, and Bulwer named him literary executor in their wills. Bulwer, writing in 1869, having known Forster for nearly forty years, described him as "A most sterling man, with an intellect at once massive and delicate. Few indeed have his strong practical sense and sound judgment; fewer still unite with such qualities his exquisite appreciation of latent beauties in literary art. Hence, in ordinary life there is no safer adviser about literary work, especially poetry; no more refined critic."[6]

Though Forster's world was populated largely by men, he knew and was respected by literary women and by the wives (and families) of his friends. Elizabeth Barrett Browning referred to him as the "ablest of English critics."[7] Jane Welsh Carlyle, who called him affectionately "Fuz" and allowed him, and only him, to seize her by the waist and swing her into a country dance at a party at Dickens's,[8] had a large and charmingly witty correspondence with Forster, as well as a warm personal friendship; Mrs. Gaskell wrote him long, friendly, sometimes frankly gossipy letters including, for example, descriptions of her first meeting with Charlotte Brontë at Haworth and of the drama over whether Charlotte would marry Mr. Nichols, and some personal reflections, not at all flattering, about the wife of John Ruskin during a rupture in that relationship.[9] Similarly with the wives and children of his many friends Forster often was an especial favorite.

Forster's own first affair of the heart is clouded in mystery even today. He apparently was secretly engaged to Laetitia Elizabeth Landon ("LEL"), a minor poet and novelist, in 1835. The plans, however formalized, collapsed after the lady's name was linked with editor William Maginn, who had a wife and four children, and with Forster's friend, the artist Daniel Maclise, and possibly even with Bulwer. Macready, who had known nothing of the impending match, records in his diary that Forster told him about it at the point of its cancellation after the lady made an "abrupt and passionate declaration of love to Maclise and on a subsequent occasion repeated it."[10]

For the next twenty years, Forster remained a confirmed bachelor, living at 58 Lincoln's Inn Fields (1834–1856), monarch, or at least prince, of his formal chambers (his rooms were the model for Tulkinghorn's in Dickens's *Bleak House*) and of his massive and always growing library. In 1856, at age forty-four, however, he married Eliza Colburn, the wife of his longtime friend, then deceased, the publisher Henry Colburn. Dickens's reaction captures the incredulity of Forster's friends at the announcement: ". . . I have the most prodigious, overwhelming, crushing, astounding, blinding, deafening, pulverizing, scarifying secret of which Forster is the hero, imaginable by the united efforts of the whole British population. It is a thing of that kind, that after I knew it (from himself) this morning, I lay down flat, as if an Engine and Tender had fallen upon me."[11] But Eliza Colburn Forster, dainty, charming, shrewd, intelligent, and very well-to-do, seems to have been an ideal mate for Forster, whom she had known many years. She assisted his work, complemented his elaborate dinner parties, and, very important, offered him support and help during his frequent ravaging illnesses.

Who, then, was John Forster and what was he like personally? As a man and as a professional he seems to have been exactly what Arthur Waugh has said of him: "Forster seemed to know everybody who wrote, and to possess everybody's confidence."[12] Bulwer agreed, and he too spoke of the personal element in the professional: "Most of my literary contemporaries are his intimate companions, and their jealousies of each other do not diminish their trust in him."[13] Arbitrary and autocratic, he was a man who could make friends and keep them, who could serve others generously, a sociable man who kept company with the great (and was proud of it), a considerate host of a man who would not let his guests best him in good talk, an influential and even powerful man who knew how to turn a common dinner with friends into a memorable event:

At the head of his table, with a number of agreeable and clever guests around him, Forster was at his best. . . . Beaming smiles, a gentle, encouraging voice, and a tenderness verging on gallantry to the ladies, took the place of the old, rough fashions. He talked ostentatiously, he *led* the talk, told most *à propos* anecdotes of the remarkable men he had met, and was fond of fortifying his own views by adding: "As Gladstone, or Guizot, or Palmerston said to me in my room," etc. But you could not but be struck by the finished shapes in which his sentences ran. There was a weight, a power of illustration, and a dramatic colouring that could only have come of long practice. He was gay, sarcastic, humorous, and it was impossible not to recognize that here was a clever man and a man of power.[14]

1812–1834. Prelude

John Forster was born April 2, 1812, at Newcastle, the eldest of four children. His father, Robert, and Uncle, "Gentleman John," were butchers; his mother, Mary, from Gallowgate, was the daughter of a dairy farmer. As a boy, Forster distinguished himself in the classics at the local grammar school, and his teachers spoke of him as their star pupil. Although described in his early teens as an "intense student of Byron and Scott—an enthusiastic antiquary and collector of Ballad poetry, and always seen with a book under his arm,"[15] he directed his first creative efforts to the drama. In 1826, the fourteen-year-old Forster adapted for the stage a two-act version of *Ali Baba or the Forty Thieves*, including speeches, stage directions, and sketches for set designs.[16]

About this time, the mother of a neighbor boy protested Forster's role in her son's love of the stage and sent the would-be playwright a pamphlet on the evils of the theater. Forster's response, "A Few Thoughts in Vindication of the Stage," constitutes a spirited defense. Drama, he insisted, aids religion: "What a reinforcement for religion and the laws, when they enter into alliances with the theatre, where the objects of contemplation are animated, where virtue and vice, happiness and misery, folly and wisdom, are exhibited in a thousand different forms; where Providence expounds its enigmas and develops all its intricacies; where the human heart, upon the rack of the passions, confesses its slightest movements; where all masks, all disguises disappear, and truth, pure and incorruptible, shines in open day."[17]

On May 2, 1828, less than a year after he penned those categorical remarks, the Newcastle Theatre staged *Charles of Tunbridge, or the Cavalier of Wildinghurst*, a drama in two acts imitative of Scott and set in the court of Charles II, by the town's precocious sixteen-year-old dramatist. "Gentleman John," a bachelor, decided that his talented nephew should receive a university education, and with his assistance, Forster entered Cambridge in October 1828. A month later, however, he withdrew to go instead to the new University College in London to study law.

Although the renowned Mr. Justice Chitty conducted Forster's legal studies and he had as school fellows, and indeed as lifelong friends, James Whiteside, later Chief Justice of the Irish Queen's Bench, and James Emerson, later Sir James Emerson Tennent, Forster was soon ambivalent about the law as his profession. Literature called, especially that of the eighteenth century, and history, specifically of the Commonwealth period. Having established himself in London to study law, Forster immediately began his career as a critic by publishing in *Newcastle Magazine* for January 1829 his "Remarks on Two of the Annuals," offering both praise and censure in what would become his typically forceful, self-assured tone.[18]

In that year, Forster met Leigh Hunt, "the first distinguished man of letters I ever knew," and the one who "influenced all my *modes* of literary thought at the outset of my life."[19] Forster revered

Hunt for viewing literature as a dignified and prestigious calling. Soon he became active in helping Hunt—both the man and the author: he joined with Edward Bulwer in 1831 to raise subscription money to publish Hunt's poetry; he wrote a preface to Hunt's *Christianism or Belief and Unbelief Reconciled* in 1832 and helped with the expenses of publication; over the years he advised him and mediated with publishers for his works and with actors and managers for his plays; he noticed each of his publications and in the mid-1830s called for public support of the man in the *New Monthly Magazine*, *Athenaeum*, and *True Sun* and later in the *Examiner*; he was largely responsible for Lord John Russell's establishing a Civil List pension for Hunt in 1847. Forster rendered this aid despite having to deal often with Hunt's famous irresponsibility and too-easily offended feelings. But in this respect, Hunt was merely the first of many literary figures proud of substantial accomplishments who clashed with the equally proud and often authoritarian critic. Indeed, a dominant and increasingly apparent element in Forster's manner has been immortalized by the London cabman who hung on Forster an epithet he was known later to quote in describing himself: "harbitrary cove."[20]

In 1831, shortly after beginning his relationship with Hunt, Forster met Charles Lamb. Like Hunt, this older man of letters helped the nineteen-year-old Forster develop lifelong attitudes about the dignity of literature as a profession. Though Lamb died within three years of the meeting, he also profoundly influenced Forster's appreciation of Shakespeare and the Elizabethan period, providing a stimulus that not only resulted in Forster's sensitive Shakespearean criticism but also in his support of efforts like those of William Charles Macready to restore to the stage the full text of the plays.[21]

Friendship with Lamb offered certain immediate practical results for the fledgling critic and student of history. Lamb's son-in-law Edward Moxon owned and published *Englishman's Magazine*. Throughout 1831, Moxon's journal provided an outlet for Forster's studies of the Commonwealth patriots John Pym, John Eliot, and Sir Henry Vane. When *Englishman's Magazine* ceased publication at the end of 1831, Moxon turned to Forster to edit a new weekly, the *Reflector*. Although the *Reflector* survived but three issues, it offered Forster valuable experience and helped increase his reputation and respect in literary circles.

Between 1831 and 1833 Forster became friends with other publishers and editors, specifically Henry Colburn and Samuel Carter Hall of the *New Monthly Magazine*, with which he became associated through Edward Bulwer (then editor) and Hunt (a contributor). Soon he was publishing reviews and occasional articles regularly in the *New Monthly Magazine*, the *Athenaeum*, and the daily *Courier*. By 1832, he had abandoned the law and determined to build a career in literature. When the seven-penny evening newspaper *True Sun* began in 1832, Forster joined as drama critic. By 1833, both the literature and the drama columns were his.

In January 1833, Forster wrote in the *True Sun* one of the earliest reviews of Tennyson, a strongly favorable evaluation of *Poems*. In general this volume received only mixed notices. Forster's full-column analysis, concluding that Tennyson was a "true poet" with the "true spirit of poetry . . . and words fit to enshrine it,"[22] demonstrates both Forster's astuteness and the manner in which he gave new writers of promise a helpful push. Tennyson is the first of several major writers of Forster's generation to receive important positive assessments from him early in their careers.

William Charles Macready, on the other hand, whom Forster also reviewed in the *True Sun*, did not need to be discovered in 1833 or to have his career pushed. Macready, actor and stage manager, had achieved the first rank in the English theater by 1820, and he retained that reputation until he retired in 1851. Forster first met Macready at the graveside of the actor Edmund Kean on May 25, 1833. By the following January, the close friendship, lasting without extended breach for forty years, had become firm. Macready's diaries offer intimate glimpses of Forster's relationships with the actor and with many important contemporaries, in particular Bulwer and Browning. Forster's name occurs more than any other in the diaries, and even a cursory perusal of the two volumes confirms their editor's assertion that Forster was Macready's "trusted counsellor and referee on almost any subject, both private and professional. . . ."[23]

Forster often placed Macready the actor or Macready the stage manager prominently in his theatrical notices, lauding most the actor's restoration to the stage of the original Shakespeare texts. Occasionally, Forster's unfailing support of Macready produced unfortunate results. His "slasher" reviews in 1836 and 1845 of the performances of Edwin Forrest, the American tragedian seen to be a rival to Macready, generated retaliatory reviews from Forrest's supporters when Macready visited America, and during Macready's final tour in 1849 a riot at the Astor Place Opera House in New York caused the deaths of seventeen persons. Similarly, when in 1837 Forster savaged the plays at Drury Lane Theatre after Macready became manager of the rival Covent Garden Theatre, very unpleasant, though not tragic, results followed (the *Age* attacked Forster personally, calling him "a butcher-boy . . . one of the Penny-a-liners of the hebdomadal Press . . . who shared not only in the management but the loss of the Covent Garden Theatre").[24]

Work on the *True Sun* provided just the right exposure, and as a result, in April 1834, Albany Fonblanque, editor of the *Examiner*, offered him the assistant-editorship of the paper and complete control of the literary and drama criticism. The opportunity was superb and he immediately resigned from the *True Sun*. John Forster, age twenty-two, had arrived. From his position with the *Examiner*, Forster produced his most important criticism; indeed from 1834 through 1855 he reigned (the word is not ill advised) as the ablest and most powerful arbiter of literary taste in England.

Early Literary Friendships

The period 1834–1843 offered Forster full and exciting involvement as critic and participant in the London Theater, and some of his best "Theatrical Examiner" columns appeared in these years. These reviews consider work by Sheridan Knowles, Charles Kean, Macready, Bulwer, and Browning. His personal relationships with men of the theater centered upon the latter three. He served them not only as critic but also as confidant, literary adviser, literary agent, mediator with publishers, actors, and theater managers, and reader of proofs.

Forster had known Edward Bulwer since 1831, when he had asked Bulwer to join in helping Leigh Hunt. His first "Literary Examiner" notice of Bulwer's work was a review of *The Last Days of Pompeii*, October 26, 1834; he then reviewed something of Bulwer's each year through 1846. In 1835 Forster played a typical role for him, arranging with Colburn to reissue Bulwer's *Pelham* as the first novel in the publisher's "Modern Novelists" series.[25] But it is his relationship with Bulwer as dramatist that best reveals Forster's versatility at this time.

He missed little of each step in the development of a Bulwer play, as he missed little in these years in the progress of Browning's two produced dramas. Generally, he offered advice and criticism during early readings with Macready, sometimes provided historical material, attended and then reviewed the production, arranged publishing details, and read proofs. Often, as with the *Sea Captain*, he acted as author's agent with the management; with *Money* in 1840, which Bulwer dedicated to him, he added supervision of the staging. The greatest rift between the two men while planning and preparing these productions occurred when Forster fell asleep during a preliminary reading of *Richelieu* at Macready's. Bulwer exploded in a letter to Macready: Forster "has warmth of feeling, but not much judgment, and wants the fine tact of good breeding."[26] Forster apologized by letter with such sincerity of feeling that Bulwer not only forgave him but thirty years later he removed the letter from its proper place in the sequence of his correspondence and placed it prominently elsewhere, writing above it a note to posterity on the strength of Forster's character: "What faults he has lie on the surface. He may be irritated, sometimes bluff to rudeness—But these are trifling irregularities in a nature solid and valuable as a block of gold. 1869."[27]

Political differences sometimes did strain their friendship, Forster always regretting Bulwer's movement away from Whig liberalism during the Corn Law and free trade controversy in the 1840s. They worked together in Dickens's amateur theatricals during the 1840s and 1850s, however, and in the 1850s in the Guild of Literature project, designed to secure life insurance for authors. Forster was extraordinarily close to Bulwer's son, Robert, in 1850 acting successfully as mediator between father and son when the latter was expelled from school for drinking, smoking, and gambling.[28] When Bulwer died in 1873, Forster was co-trustee of his estate with Robert, and he helped see a new edition of Bulwer's novels through the press shortly thereafter. Three years later, when Forster died, Robert, by then Second Lord Lytton and Viceroy of India, wrote: "I feel quite bewildered. All my courage is gone. He was father, brother, and more, much more, to me. No man ever *had* such a friend as I had in him."[29]

During the period in the late 1830s when Forster was involved in Bulwer's plays, he and Macready were equally active in producing the work of Robert Browning. Forster had first reviewed Browning

in 1835. Indeed the poet never forgot that praise for him and his
newest work, the first published under his name—*Paracelsus*. Forster
had concluded his strongly positive evaluation: ". . . we may safely
predict for him a brilliant career, if he continues true to the present
promise of his genius. He possesses all the elements of a fine poet."[30]
Paracelsus received some sharp criticism and Browning, who had
hoped for critical acclaim at that time, hard upon the disappoint-
ment of *Pauline* in 1833, recalled Forster's words more than once
when referring to him as "my early Understander." Writing to
Forster in 1875, in the last letter between them (Forster would be
dead in two months), Browning tells of speaking to a friend of a
new generation who believed that *Paracelsus* had been warmly received: "I told the true story of everybody's silence or condemnation
till the *Examiner* spoke up for it. So long as my poems last they
will continue to record that fact and its consequences—their fitting
preface."[31]

These two men, born twenty-two days apart (Forster the older),
knew each other for forty years. They met on New Year's Eve 1835
at Macready's and by February 1, 1836, Macready records that
Browning is Forster's "all-in-all." During 1835 and 1836 Forster
praised Browning's work in the *Examiner*, and in an article for *New
Monthly Magazine* (March 1836), "Evidences of a New Genius for
Dramatic Poetry," he singled out Browning for special praise.

As in the case with Bulwer and Forster, Macready's diaries for
these years offer many glimpses of powerful disputes among the
three—Macready, Browning, and Forster—during the planning,
revising, and production of Browning's plays, *Strafford* (1837) and
A Blot in the 'Scutcheon (1843). Forster probably suggested Strafford
as a dramatic subject; he had just completed, with Browning's help,
a biography of Strafford. Forster particularly insisted that Macready
produce the play, and he superintended its several revisions. He
reviewed as favorably as he could what turned out to be a feeble
production, as Macready had all along feared, but the review did
not satisfy Browning.

Through the 1840s and 1850s Forster issued generally favorable
reviews of Browning's works (except for *Sordello*, which he generously
ignored). He supervised publication of much of the work of both
Brownings, Robert and Elizabeth Barrett. From the middle 1840s
until at least the mid-1860s, relations between the two men were
stable and warm. Through the 1850s, when the Brownings lived

in Italy, the tone of the letters is not only cordial but occasionally nostalgic ("those old days, Forster—at your rooms—then the play; then the projects!" [1854]);[32] in 1861, we find strong evidence of Browning's regard for Forster in a thousand-word description of the exact circumstances of Elizabeth Barrett Browning's death and burial. Forster is asked to share these details with any of Browning's concerned friends in London.[33]

Back in England in the 1860s, the poet fell into the habit of dining with Forster each Sunday; Forster considered this meeting a rule, but it soon strained the nerves of Browning, who often viewed Forster as "patronizing." Cordial relations actually ceased at another dinner, not at Forster's, after the critic had taken exception to the poet's having accepted the veracity of a certain lady: "Suddenly, Browning became very fierce, and said, 'Dare to say one word in disparagement of that Lady'—seizing a decanter while he spoke—'and I will pitch this bottle of claret at your head!' "[34] Peace restored, efforts to effect reconciliation failed. This breach lasted until just prior to Forster's death in 1876.

Dating from the period when he first began working with Macready, Bulwer, and Browning, Forster had an intense and important, albeit comparatively short-lived, friendship with William Harrison Ainsworth, prolific novelist and publisher. Ainsworth liked Forster and said so publicly in the preface to his historical novel *Crichton* (1836), where he describes Forster as "this youthful historian . . . [who] is a subtle analyser of character—a profound and philosophical thinker," concluding, "Je suis l'ami de Forster."[35] Indeed, during the years 1836–1839, Ainsworth, Forster, and also Dickens were largely inseparable—partying, horseback riding, walking, and traveling as constant companions. Ainsworth introduced Forster to Dickens on Christmas Day 1836. The introduction of Forster and Dickens initiated one of the most intimate and fruitful friendships in the annals of English literary history, enduring without a serious breach until the novelist's death in 1870.

The friendship with Dickens developed rapidly. Like so many others, Dickens soon depended heavily on Forster's advice and help. Forster would say later that from October 1837, less than a year after they had met, he read in manuscript or proof everything that Dickens wrote. Of course he accorded the novelist ample space in the "Literary Examiner" columns. From February 28, 1836, to December 22, 1855, he published forty-six reviews of Dickens's works, five extracts from the novels, and eight articles on related subjects (such as two articles by Dickens on copyright); further, in 1850, he mentioned *Household Words*, Dickens's weekly periodical, in eighteen articles and in 1851, in nineteen.[36] Although not generally known at the time, evidence does exist suggesting that Forster continued to review for the *Examiner* each of Dickens's novels, even after he had apparently given up all writing of periodical criticism at the end of 1855.[37]

About the time he took control of seeing Dickens's writings through the press, Forster became chief literary adviser to Chapman and Hall, then publishing *Pickwick Papers*. Arthur Waugh, historian of the firm's first hundred years, indicates that Forster pursued his duties with typical energy: "It was not long before Forster was acting as literary adviser to the house, swinging into the office as though the whole place belonged to him, and carrying off the proof of half the publications, to read at leisure in his chambers."[38]

That Forster was no stranger to publishing houses and to negotiating with publishers served Dickens well almost immediately. Forster's first specifically financial assistance to Dickens involved extricating the novelist from contracts he had signed with Macrone and Bentley, agreements entered into before the enormous success of *Pickwick* had caused the economic value of Dickens's works to soar.

Dickens had given Macrone copyright of his first published book, *Sketches by Boz*, for £100; further, he had agreed to provide Macrone with a novel. After witnessing the incredible success of *Pickwick*, Macrone decided to reissue the *Sketches* in monthly installments and green wrappers, precisely imitating the *Pickwick* numbers. Dickens, furious, sent Forster to negotiate. Macrone remained firm at first, finally yielding but refusing to accept less than £2000 for the copyright. Forster was appalled but reported to Dickens, and Chapman and Hall. Though not on hand when the final decision was demanded, Forster readily agreed in the end when Chapman and Hall closed the deal with Macrone at £2250. Macrone died before the issue of whether Dickens owed him a novel could be settled.

With Bentley, Dickens committed himself to much more, and Forster's work was substantially more difficult. Dickens had agreed to be editor of *Bentley's Miscellany*, in which *Oliver Twist* appeared monthly, and to produce, for £750 each, two additional novels. Through a series of complicated and ultimately very unfriendly stages, Forster managed to free Dickens of the editorship—turned over to Ainsworth—to have one of the promised novels dropped, to repurchase the rights to *Oliver Twist* with the remaining stock and the Cruikshank plates, and to have Chapman and Hall buy out Bentley's claim to the second novel, *Barnaby Rudge*, which had been promised Bentley by late 1838 but never delivered. With these negotiations completed, Dickens became entirely free to publish solely with Chapman and Hall. Forster continued to work for his friend with the firm and arranged for Dickens to have a greater share in the profits and the return of copyright to himself for each of his books after five years.[39]

Despite the enormous amounts of time occupied with writing his weekly columns and his occasional pieces for other journals, and the time spent developing his professional and social friendships, Forster never lost sight of what he always believed to be his most important work—writing historical, and later literary, biographies. Hence, when approached in 1835 by Dr. Dionysius Lardner to contribute to his *Cabinet Cyclopedia* biographies of "Eminent British Statesmen," Forster gladly accepted. Professor Lardner apparently had seen some of Forster's writing while he was attending University College and undoubtedly had seen in 1831 his articles on the Commonwealth figures in *Englishman's Magazine*. Forster contributed five volumes to the *Cyclopedia*: Sir John Eliot and Thomas Wentworth, Earl of Strafford (1836); John Pym and John Hampden (1837); Henry Vane and Henry Marten (1838); and Oliver Cromwell (two volumes, 1839). In 1840, Longmans published an edition called *Statesmen of the Commonwealth*, with Forster's introduction, "A Treatise on Popular Progress in English History, Being an Introduction to the Study of the Great Civil War in the Seventeenth Century," which also appeared as a separate work in 1840. These studies established Forster's reputation as the leading modern historian of the Commonwealth period.

A controversy surrounding the first of these volumes, on Eliot and Strafford, casts light on Forster's and his contemporaries' attitudes about authorship. The lives of Eliot and Strafford were due to Lardner in May 1836. But Forster's father died in February 1836, after the Eliot material had been finished but before the completion of the Strafford section. At this juncture, Browning apparently stepped in to assist Forster in successfully meeting his deadline. When the volume appeared, Browning's contribution went unacknowledged, but soon thereafter, Forster aided Browning with his play *Strafford* (1837). This comfortable arrangement, which suited the two friends, unfortunately has created problems for later literary historians desirous of establishing the canon of each author's work, and some partisans have been very aggressive. In 1892, F. J. Furnival and the London Browning Society went so far as to reprint separately the Strafford material in Forster's volume as *Robert Browning's Prose Life of Strafford*, the implication being that while Forster had done the research, the writing was pure Browning. In our own time, DeVane has doubted the implied magnitude of Browning's contribution, but the controversy is far from settled, its most recent stimulus coming from the printing of a Forster letter exclaiming, "Browning finishes Strafford!"—a revelation which really adds nothing new.[40]

Important perspective on Forster's relationship with Browning as collaborator is available through a brief glance at two subsequent instances when Forster attempted to set up an anonymous collaboration, the first with Bulwer in 1840, the second with Ainsworth in 1842. Forster wrote to Bulwer asking his help in a book about the Queen Anne period and suggesting that Bulwer tackle the political portions—"scenes in the Commons and the Lords, and the Closet of the Queen," and including specifically "the Bolingbrokes and Oxfords, the Marlboroughs, Godolphins, and Somersets, the Shaftesburys, Whartons, and Sunderlands, Anne herself and her husband, Masham, Sarah Marlborough and the Lords, Sacheveral and his mobs." For himself: "I would take . . . the more literary portions, the Swifts and Popes, Defoes and Steeles, Pryors and Gays, the Vanbrughs, Congreves, Knellers, Booths, and Bettertons. I do not propose that *my own name should at all appear in the first edition*, though the separate hands in the work might be marked as seemed best to you."[41]

With Ainsworth, the proposal was more humanitarian and decidedly less ambitious. Aware of the strain that Ainsworth was under in 1842 editing *Ainsworth's Magazine* and serializing in it his novel *The Miser's Daughter*, Forster acted with compassion and dispatch when he heard that Ainsworth's mother had died in the middle of March with the announced beginning of the novelist's *Windsor Castle* but two weeks away. Forster offered: "Is there anything I can write for you? I imagine that you will defer the *Windsor Castle* this month— but should you not do so, I might be of some assistance to you. I have all of my Henry VIII books here, and if you told me some particular thing you wanted—it may be horrible conceit—but somehow I think I might be of some beggarly service to you."[42]

Although neither proposal developed, each mitigates any wonder that Forster did not openly acknowledge Browning's help with the life of Strafford. Of course, Forster was himself well used to anonymous work; virtually all of his criticism was unsigned. That anonymity never suggested to him a lessening of quality, however, is clear not only in his own writing but in the suggestions to both Bulwer and Ainsworth: he wanted to do the book on Queen Anne; for the best volume possible he thought Bulwer's help indispensable and was willing to give Bulwer full credit if that would induce him to provide his valuable part. With Ainsworth, we find not only Forster's friendship recorded in the letter but also respect for Ainsworth's commitments to his public and to the well-being of his journal. The generosity of Forster's proposals is characteristic of him, and we can only regret that the full extent of the aid he offered his contemporaries behind the scenes, amply suggested by testimonials from many in their later years, can never be precisely identified.

Although Ainsworth did not ask Forster to use his books on Henry VIII to assist with *Windsor Castle*, another of Forster's most important contemporaries, originally attracted to the young historian by his two-volume *Oliver Cromwell* in 1839, was at that time using much of Forster's private research and library material to aid in his own writings, particularly on Cromwell. This man, Thomas Carlyle, was himself an historian. Forster had written positively of Carlyle's *French Revolution* in 1837 and had praised and followed in detail Carlyle's series of lectures in 1838. For his part, the older man had enjoyed "Strafford" in the *Cyclopedia* and even more the two volumes on the Protector. Carlyle made the first friendly overture, asking Forster for his support in the *Examiner* of a project to finance a new lending library in London. The support was gladly given; the library project succeeded. Carlyle was soon not only enjoying Forster's company for serious historical discussions but also, as has been suggested, he was borrowing Forster's materials and books, seeking his advice, and to some extent accepting his criticism as his own work on Cromwell developed. Their friendship lasted nearly forty years, ceasing only with Forster's death.

Forster reviewed Carlyle's work regularly and favorably, that routine suffering only one hitch in 1850—with the reactionary *Latter-Day Pamphlets*, which Forster stopped reviewing individually after the third had appeared. Forster provided Carlyle many of the same services he offered other friends: representing him with publishers, advising him on financial matters, and assisting him with his research, especially in the five years leading to Carlyle's *Oliver Cromwell's Letters and Speeches* (1845). The letters between the two men are warm, brimming with ideas, and full of references to important contemporaries, many of whom were mutual friends: Browning, Bulwer, Dickens, Emerson, FitzGerald, Froude, Landor, Macready, Mill, Milnes, and Tennyson. Carlyle respected Forster's work in history and biography, and praised the *Statesmen of the Commonwealth*, *The Life and Adventures of Oliver Goldsmith*, and the "Lives" of Landor and Dickens. Of the three-volume *Life of Charles Dickens*, Carlyle told Forster: "[you] have performed a feat which, except in Boswell, the unique, I know not where to parallel. So long as Dickens is interesting to his fellow-men, here will be seen face to face, what Dickens's manner of existing was."[43]

The strength of the friendship between these two men may be best illustrated by considering Forster's relationship with Jane Welsh Carlyle. She called him "Fuz," and letters between Forster and Jane Carlyle are often delightful, and on her part, full of the ironic, often sarcastic, wit and humor, which were her hallmark. She smoothed the way between husband and friend during the brief coolness over the *Latter-Day Pamphlets*. When she died alone in her coach on the way home from lunch at the Forsters' while Carlyle was in Scotland, Forster immediately attended not only to the obvious details but also to those most sensitive and important to Carlyle: ". . . had it not been for John Forster and Dr. Quain, and everybody's mercy to me, there must have been, by rule, a coroner's inquest held, which would have been a blotch upon my memory, intolerable then, and discordantly ugly for all time coming. It is to Forster's unwearied and invincible efforts that I am indebted for escape from this sad defilement of my feelings."[44] Carlyle later intended one final office for Forster regarding his wife. When giving his biographer, Froude, all of his own and Jane Carlyle's papers and letters, he told Froude to seek the advice after his death of his brother, John, and of Forster before publishing the sensitive private materials of his wife—which detailed the unhappiness she had experienced in her marriage. Forster died five years before Carlyle, though after having read the Jane Carlyle materials and having admired Carlyle's decision to permit publication.[45] Forster's death naturally precluded his serving as Carlyle's literary executor and his advising Froude, as his friend had hoped.

At the end of the 1830s, then, Forster had developed the important friendships of his life and had begun, too, his most important writing. He had been in London for ten years, and, at age twenty-eight, he was a figure of extraordinary accomplishment. His workload was prodigious. Between January 1, 1834, and October 1, 1841, Forster wrote 816 articles.[46] In the *Examiner* alone for the last three months of 1840 and all of 1841, he wrote fifty articles for the "Literary Examiner" and twenty for the "Theatrical Examiner."[47] His friend Whitwell Elwin described his work life at this time:

. . . the reading which his book-reviewing involved consumed more of his time than the composition of his articles. His theatrical criticisms broke in upon his evening hours, which were constantly spent at the play. These regular engagements did not yield him a sufficient income, and he had to swell his earnings by miscellaneous essays. . . . He read manuscripts for . . . friends who already confided in the soundness of his judgment. . . . He had a big correspondence . . . and was punctilious not to leave letters unanswered, nor to delay his replies. With all these obstructions . . . it was an obstacle the more that his inclination was for political and literary biographies which required elaborate research. . . . [He] cast aside his journalistic duties from Saturday morning to Tuesday, and . . . [devoted] the interval to productions of greater pith. The process to most men would have been disheartening or impossible. . . . But Forster was perfect in . . . self-control. He would go to his writing at any odd moment, and concentrate his whole attention upon it, undisturbed by the distractions which had immediately preceded and were presently to follow. This power of living exclusively in the actual moment attended him in his diversions as in his industries.[48]

The 1840s. Journalism and the Literary Jungle

Forster began the 1840s involved principally in journalism, and for the most part he confined his writing to periodicals and newspapers. He wrote no book-length study between 1839 *(Cromwell)* and 1848 *(The Life and Adventures of Oliver Goldsmith)*. Although most of his work appeared in the *Examiner*, he wrote also for the *Foreign*

Quarterly Review, the *Edinburgh Review*, *Douglas Jerrold's Shilling Magazine*, and the *Daily News*.

In April 1842, Forster, still assistant editor of the *Examiner*, became the anonymous editor of the *Foreign Quarterly Review*, a position he held, retaining his anonymity, until July 1843. Some of his writing for this periodical doubtless has yet to be identified, but we do know that he used the secrecy he enjoyed to write at least two articles rather intemperately attacking the American newspaper press; his motives included a personal interest in the fight for better copyright laws and in the particular anguish Dickens had been suffering from American book publishers appropriating his work. Several years earlier the copyright laws in England had been altered favorably for authors, and Forster had been active in pushing for the changes. In 1841 also appeared the *Pic Nic Papers*, a volume edited by Dickens and designed to raise funds for Macrone's widow and children. Forster's contribution was an article written as a dialogue, "John Dryden and Jacob Tonson," offering praise for Dryden as a man of honor who earned his living as a professional author, thereby lending dignity and prestige to that profession. But the negative portrait of Tonson the publisher when contrasted with that of Dryden makes clear that the author-publisher relationship was much in Forster's mind at this time. The fierceness of his anger and the prospect of anonymity allowed his attacks in the *Foreign Quarterly Review* to exceed acceptable limits, and these articles fail as notable examples of Forster's craft.[49]

The work on Dryden shows the depth of Forster's interest in the role and position of the professional author and also in literary figures of the eighteenth century; indeed, the men of letters in the generations immediately following Dryden occupied Forster continually over the period 1844–1855. Although he wrote two essays for the *Foreign Quarterly Review* on Socrates and Plato, respectively, and "A History for Young England," for *Douglas Jerrold's Shilling Magazine*, his long biographical sketches of Charles Churchill and Daniel Defoe in the *Edinburgh Review* in 1845 are more characteristic of the direction his research activities took at this time, culminating in his full-length study *The Life and Adventures of Oliver Goldsmith* in 1848.

Forster's tenure as editor of the *Foreign Quarterly Review* was brief, and, as has been suggested, in his occasional intemperateness, not always worthy of him as a serious critic and journalist. His next role as editor was distinctly unsatisfactory, almost as much so as it was unsought for. In January 1846, Dickens, disregarding Forster's advice, set out to edit a new liberal paper, the *Daily News*, against great odds, including the opposition of the *Times*. Within three weeks, Dickens had resigned as editor, and Forster, who had signed on with his friend to write political leaders, suddenly found himself in the editor's chair. Forster now struggled, at a very busy time in his own life, with full responsibility for a daily paper. Soon this burden and some management changes convinced him to withdraw, and he resigned in October 1846. For the next year, Forster produced no journalism except for the *Examiner*, devoting the remainder of his time to his *Oliver Goldsmith*.

In November 1847, however, the opportunity arrived to become an editor under favorable conditions and without any question of anonymity. That month Albany Fonblanque turned over to Forster the complete editorship of the *Examiner*, and until 1856 Forster alone was responsible for the paper's contents. He wrote most of the political leaders himself and continued writing many of the literary and theatrical columns, but with help in the latter cases. These were dramatic times for England, and in the years of his editorship Forster wrote leaders on such important subjects as free trade, educational reform, Irish problems, ecclesiastical reform, the restoration of the Catholic hierarchy, revolution on the Continent, the Crimean War, and domestic politics.[50] In charge of obtaining the services of others, Forster managed to secure articles from Tennyson, Dickens, Landor, and Carlyle, to name just a few persons from whom he printed multiple offerings.

In addition to his journalism, Forster continued in the 1840s to support the literary interest of his friends, especially Dickens. He continued to superintend the production of each of the novelist's works and to offer advice during the writing (much of this advice is preserved in correspondence, Dickens being often abroad in these years). Forster arranged for the famous "performance" of *The Chimes* in 1844 when Dickens returned to London from Italy just to try out a reading of the story on close friends. When Dickens began his amateur theatricals in 1845 to raise charitable contributions for needy literary figures, Forster played Kitely to Dickens's Bobadil in Jonson's *Every Man in His Humour* (the most successful of the group's ultimately varied repertoire), and Forster even adapted in 1846 Fletcher's *Elder Brother*, adding a life of the author and a new prologue and epilogue.

Forster's most signficant achievement of the 1840s was *The Life and Adventures of Oliver Goldsmith*, which appeared in March 1848. Ten years in the writing, the volume was dedicated to Dickens, "a fellow Goldsmithian," and contained seven-hundred gilt-edged pages and thirty-five illustrations by various artist-friends. Reviewers welcomed the book, including Bulwer in the *Edinburgh Review*, and Dickens in private letters praised the volume for the dignity it bestowed on the profession of literature, a comment that could only have pleased Forster very much. A brief flap did occur when Sir James Prior charged that Forster had appropriated material from Prior's two-volume *Life* of 1836, but the controversy was defused not only by Forster, who explained how he had gathered and used his materials, but also by the reviewers who agreed that facts discovered by Prior should be available to all subsequent biographers of Goldsmith, and finally by Washington Irving in his preface to a revised edition of Goldsmith's works. Irving describes Prior's volumes as "cumbrous" and "overlaid with details"; Forster's were "elegant and discursive pages . . . executed with a spirit, a feeling, a grace, and an elegance that leaves little to be desired."[51] These words must have lived long in Forster's memory but not nearly as long as Dickens's personal homage: "I desire no better for my fame, when my personal dustiness shall be past the controul (*sic*) of my love of order, than such a biographer and such a critic."[52]

Forster's concern for the dignity of literature as a profession predated, of course, the publication of *Oliver Goldsmith*; we have noted it in his earliest views of Hunt and Lamb. Bulwer, in fact, had proposed a plan for a "literary loan and life insurance society" in his "Monthly Commentary" in the *New Monthly Magazine* for March 1833.[53] In the late 1830s Forster had joined with Thomas Noon Talfourd, Bulwer, and Benjamin Disraeli in supporting a new copyright law. The issue became heated some few years after Forster's articles in the *Foreign Quarterly Review* against the American newspaper press, when, in 1847, Thackeray satirized Bulwer and Forster in his series of parodies of contemporary authors called *"Punch's* Prize Novelists."* Forster was angered by the attack on Bulwer, and to a lesser extent by that on himself, but principally he objected to Thackeray's poking fun at fellow professionals.

Forster probably first met Thackeray about 1834, and by 1836 he had reviewed six of Thackeray's works. In 1840, when Thackeray wrote expressing doubt about the prospects of *The Paris Sketch Book* and asking Forster's help, four columns of the *Examiner* explored reasons for reader satisfaction with the volume. While editor of the *Foreign Quarterly Review* Forster published at least eight articles by Thackeray.[54] Nevertheless, Thackeray's opposition to government pensions for professional authors and his coolness toward discussions of the need to raise the prestige of the literary profession set him at odds with Forster on an important matter of principle. The parodies in *Punch* caused Forster to observe in a private conversation that Thackeray was "false as hell,"[55] a comment that, when made known to Thackeray, caused the novelist to snub the critic. Dickens and others patched up the breach but relations remained strained during the next several years: in 1850, Thackeray in the *Morning Chronicle* and Forster in the *Examiner* disputed these issues as well as the claim that Thackeray had "a disposition to pay court to the non-literary class by disparaging his fellow labourers";[56] in 1851, Thackeray closed his lectures on "English Humourists of the Eighteenth Century" with an emphatic protestation that society did not despise the writing profession; consistently he opposed and spoke disapprovingly of the initiation by Dickens, Bulwer, and Forster of a second series of amateur theatricals to raise contributions for the Guild of Literature and Art, a society the three men hoped would offer financial help to authors in need in a way similar to that suggested by Bulwer seventeen years earlier.

Forster and Thackeray were not always at odds, however, even during this period. Forster generally reviewed Thackeray's works positively, though often qualifying his praise of the novels, such as *Vanity Fair*, by bemoaning their darkness and characterization, which disallowed even the most virtuous member of the cast to appear without some serious blemish. The personal relations of the two men could be at times quite cordial. In 1849, for example, when Thackeray was seriously ill, Forster visited almost daily; he even brought with him his personal physician, whom Thackeray later credited with his cure.[57] Nevertheless, the relationship disintegrated in 1858, when Forster sided with Dickens in support of the young Edmund Yates, who had insulted Thackeray in a hastily written sketch published in *Town Talk*. This incident followed closely Thackeray's unfortunate observation (later publicly quoted) that a young actress and not Dickens's sister-in-law, Georgina, was responsible for the breakup of Dickens's marriage.

Because it touches both favorably and unfavorably upon the dignity-of-literature issue, some discussion of Forster's relationship with Tennyson is appropriate here. Forster, it will be recalled, approved Tennyson's poetry in 1833. In 1842, he wrote the first important notice of Tennyson's new volumes. When, in October 1845, Tennyson was awarded a Civil List Pension of £200 a year, Forster believed him worthy of such an honor although it meant that Sheridan Knowles, another candidate for the pension, would be passed over. Bulwer, unsympathetic to Tennyson, used the supposed slighting of Knowles to satirize Tennyson as "School-Miss Alfred" in his poem "The New Timon," published anonymously. While Bulwer denied to Forster any knowledge of the poem's authorship, Forster recognized Bulwer's hand, and when Tennyson asked Forster if Bulwer were not the satirist, Forster confirmed Tennyson's suspicions. Tennyson's reaction was to respond to Bulwer in kind; he wrote "The New Timon and the Poets," in part describing Bulwer as a "Lion" who "shook a mane en papillotes" (curl papers).[58] He sent the lines to Forster, who persuaded Tennyson to allow them to be published, arguing that justice exceeded the claims of friendship. Through an intermediary Forster sent the lines to *Punch*, where they appeared under the pseudonym Alcibiades. Tennyson very shortly regretted his retort (later he would deny giving Forster permission to publish) and sent to *Punch* "An Afterthought," apologizing for his bitter response and asserting that silence would have been the better action. Bulwer and Tennyson reconciled later, and Bulwer deleted the offending passages when reprinting the poem. Here, then, is a literary adventure wherein no one, except at the end, behaved with dignity. Forster's part in the affair parallels his overreaction to the American press, where righteous indignation led him into excess.

Despite Forster's role in this temporary unpleasantness, the relationship between him and Tennyson remained on friendly terms through the 1850s, with Tennyson living for a time in 1854 at 60 Lincoln's Inn Fields, next door to Forster at number 58.[59] In the early 1850s Tennyson contributed political poems to the *Examiner*, where in December 1854 "The Charge of the Light Brigade" first appeared. Within a year a chaplain in the Crimea wrote asking for copies of the poem, which was then enjoying a tremendous success among the soldiers. Tennyson, understandably proud and eager to respond, had to face the fact that he had altered the poem the soldiers had come to relish. He turned to Forster, sending him the original version and a specific, impassioned request: "For heaven's sake get *this* copy fairly printed at once, and sent out . . . and see that there are *no mistakes*; and I will be bound to you for evermore and more than ever."[60] Regrettably the closeness suggested by Tennyson's request and his expression of gratitude did not survive the mid-1860s. A disagreement over one of Forster's dinner invitations resulted in their meeting less and less after that time during the few occasions each year that Tennyson visited London.

The 1850s. The Height of His Powers

Returning to the issue of the dignity of Literature as a profession, we find Forster at the beginning of the 1850s heavily involved with Dickens in the amateur theatricals planned to support the Guild of Literature and Art as well as in the initiation of *Household Words*, Dickens's weekly magazine. Forster, Dickens, and Bulwer struggled throughout the 1850s to merge the Guild of Literature and Art with the Royal Literary Fund, which to these three "reformers" seemed stodgy, patronizing, and underrepresentative of contemporary professional writers who might make it efficient, expand its functions, and broaden its membership. Their efforts failed and not even Forster's offer to bequeath his vast personal library to the fund, if it would liberalize some of its practices, produced any effect; indeed, after having his offer rejected in 1859, Forster resigned.[61]

The decade of the 1850s held other disappointments. His affiliation with *Household Words*, which began with much promise, ended in frustration. Initially, Forster owned one-eighth share in the magazine, acted as its business adviser, arranged for the appointment of the invaluable W. H. Wills as subeditor, provided occasional literary articles, and helped compile the "Household Narrative of Current Events." But during these years, Dickens grew close to the young novelist Wilkie Collins and less attached to his old friend. Wills proved so effective a manager that Forster found himself less consulted than he would have liked. In 1856, he gave up his interest in *Household Words*,[62] and, in fact, at this time he gave over virtually all of his journalistic enterprises. No break occurred with Dickens, however, for in 1857 the novelist sought Forster's counsel on the advisability of beginning paid public reading tours and, more important, in 1858 Dickens made Forster and not Collins the confidant

in Dickens's impending separation from his wife of twenty-two
years. Forster opposed the readings, interestingly on the grounds
that it would be a lowering of the dignity of his profession for a
literary artist to become a "professional showman."[63] Forster advised, too, against Dickens's public statement in *Household Words*
and in *Punch* describing the separation from his wife, advice Dickens
would have done well to heed. In the legal separation agreements,
Forster represented Dickens. Hence, at the close of this decade
Forster found himself, as always, at the center of a friend's problem;
privy to the most intimate details and understandably reluctant, he
nevertheless proved a characteristically able, discreet, and reliable
friend.

   Not unexpectedly, Forster's published work in the 1850s, beyond
his criticism, turned to figures of the seventeenth and eighteenth
centuries. He began by anonymously editing and providing footnotes for an edition of the *Diaries of John Evelyn*, 1850–1852; these
were reprinted in 1854 and 1857, the latter with Forster's preface.
In 1854 he edited the third edition of *Some Memorials of John Hampden*
by his old friend Lord Nugent, of whom he appended a lengthy
memoir. In the same year appeared his revised and expanded *Life
and Times of Oliver Goldsmith* (two volumes); its popularity necessitated a second edition in 1855. A long biographical portrait of
Samuel Foote appeared in the *Quarterly Review* in September 1854,
and in March 1855, also in the *Quarterly*, he published a monograph
on Sir Richard Steele. He returned to Oliver Cromwell in January
1856, publishing in the *Edinburgh Review* "The Civil Wars and
Oliver Cromwell." In 1858 he published in two volumes his *Historical and Biographical Essays* including, now expanded, his earlier
biographies of Churchill, Defoe, Foote, and Steele, "The Civil Wars
and Oliver Cromwell," and, for the first time, "The Debates on the
Grand Remonstrance" and "The Plantagenets and Tudors, a Sketch
of Constitutional History."

   So incredible a writing effort required relief from his traditionally
heavy schedule. That relief came in January 1856 when he turned
over the editorship of the *Examiner* to Henry Morley and left the
paper for the first time in nearly a quarter of a century. The immediate cause of this momentous action was his appointment as
Secretary of the Lunacy Commission on December 28, 1855, with
an annual salary of £800.[64] The break with the *Examiner* must have
touched Forster deeply; certainly it moved his longtime employer

and good friend, Albany Fonblanque, as he attempted to respond to Forster's letter of resignation:

> I cannot deny the wisdom of your determination, though all other cir-
> cumstances of it, the straightforwardness, the kindness, the frankness,
> make it only the more unacceptable to me. . . . You may see by the
> erasures that my eyes and hand are not very true and steady and, in truth,
> I write with a heavy heart. The breaking of a tie at my time of life is a
> sad thing. We have been connected now for twenty-three years, and have
> never had a difference beyond opinion—seldom that—never unfriendly.
> Be your successor who he may, he can never fill your place. I feel that
> my moorings are lifted.[65]

Fonblanque later would say of Forster and his *Examiner* criticisms:
". . . although the wide popularity of his more permanent and
solid works has eclipsed the fame of his critical essays on books and
the drama, those who remember the 'Examiner' in its palmiest days
cannot have forgotten how eagerly authors and actors awaited its
verdict upon their merits, and how confidently this was accepted
by the public."[66]

The 1850s were, then, times of great activity for Forster, but
also times of great change and undoubtedly some nostalgia: his
health, never good, deteriorated (he was in bed several months in
1853 with rheumatic fever); Ainsworth left London and Macready
retired and did the same; Browning was abroad; Bulwer moved away
politically; Dickens moved toward Collins and younger friends and
not only away from Forster but also from heeding his advice; the
hectic days at the *Examiner* came to an end, to be replaced by an
entirely different set of duties.[67] Yet Forster was free finally—for a
time—to devote himself to historical studies, those pursuits he
himself always believed would be the basis for posterity's judgment.

1861–1876. Final Responsibilities

The 1860s opened promisingly enough. Forster was made Commissioner in Lunacy in 1861, with an increase in his annual salary
to £1500. Following this good fortune he had built in 1862 and
thereafter occupied an enormous mansion, Palace Gate, near Kensington Gardens. Later, in 1867 he was awarded an honorary Doctor
of Laws degree from Trinity College, Dublin (Forster had been called
to the Bar in 1843 but never actually practiced law). Further, his

historical research continued to prosper. In 1860 he published *Arrest of the Five Members by Charles the First* and *The Debates on the Grand Remonstrance, November and December, 1641*, with an "Introductory Essay on English Freedom under the Plantagenet and Tudor Sovereigns." In 1864 he expanded his earlier biographical study of Sir John Eliot to two volumes. He was well into plans for a similar expansion of his Strafford materials when the death of Walter Savage Landor interrupted his progress; in fact from this point on Forster published no historical writing. The last twelve years of his life (1864–1876), indeed, were marked by ill health, few new or close friendships—that with Whitwell Elwin, editor of the *Quarterly Review* 1863–1870, being a notable exception—hard work, a good bit of which was unappreciated by his contemporaries, and the passing of old comrades. The deaths of Landor (1864), Alexander Dyce (1869), Dickens (1870), and Bulwer (1873) and, subsequently, his work on their biographies or their collected editions or both of these (in Landor's case) consumed most of his energy after 1865.

The relationship with Landor deserves special consideration, going back as it did almost thirty years. Forster first met Landor in 1836 at the specific request of the poet. Landor had been pleased by two of Forster's notices of him in 1834: in the *Examiner* review of his *Citation and Examination of William Shakespeare* and in the *New Monthly Magazine* series "Evidences of a New Genius for Dramatic Poetry,"[68] which, as we have seen, also praised the young Robert Browning.

The meeting with Landor was auspicious for both men. It provided Forster an entrée into Lady Blessington's salon, where he soon became an intimate and undoubtably enjoyed the prestige afforded by that contact; it gave Landor a friend for the rest of his long life, a badly needed editor, adviser, business and literary agent, helpful critic, literary executor, and biographer. Although Landor was sixty-one and Forster but twenty-four when they met, the relationship grew rapidly; from 1838 until 1856 Landor, who lived mainly in Bath, moved in with Forster each year when visiting London, and the two men usually spent Landor's birthday at Bath. By the mid-1840s Landor, who had turned the publication of all his work over to Forster, was suggesting that Forster might one day superintend a collected edition of his works and write a biography.[69]

Forster faithfully accomplished both projects but the latter only with severe strain. The youthful Forster had been attracted to Landor through their mutual love for classical antiquity and the young man's appreciation of the older's radicalism. Unfortunately, Forster grew more conservative, more proper, more typically a representative of middle-class values and middle-class morality, and certain of Landor's scandalous activities, such as the abandoning of his wife and children and his problems with libel, presented difficulties for Forster in his role as biographer. For these reasons and because many persons involved in Landor's life were still alive, Forster struggled for nearly five years, until 1869, to finish both volumes of Landor's "Life." The final product was unquestionably less than satisfactory.

Completion of the Landor volumes and a memoir of Dyce, another longtime friend and Shakespeare scholar, appended to the catalog of the Dyce collection now at the Victoria and Albert Museum, was followed in June 1870 by the death of Dickens. That he would write Dickens's biography was understood, and his labor began immediately. The first volume appeared in 1872 and the third and final one in 1874. During these years, Forster's health, unstable at least since the mid-1840s, troubled him, and in 1872 he had to resign as Commissioner in Lunacy. His friend Percy Fitzgerald offered a moving description of Forster's physical struggles during this period:

Forster's latter days, that is, I suppose, for some seven or eight years, were an appalling state of martyrdom; no words could paint it. It was gout in its most terrible form, that is, on the chest. This malady was due, in the first place, to his early hard life, when rest and hours of sleep were neglected or set at nought. Too good living also was accountable. He loved good cheer and had an excellent taste in wines, fine clarets, etc. Such things were fatal to his complaint. This gout took the shape of an almost eternal cough, which scarcely ever left him. It began invariably with the night and kept him awake, the water rising on his chest and overpowering him.[70]

While Forster was at work on the *Life of Dickens*, Bulwer died, and Forster began helping Robert Lytton with a new edition of his father's novels even while Landor's collected works and eight of the nine volumes of Dyce's third edition of Shakespeare were in preparation.

Incredibly, despite virtually immobilizing ill-health, Forster, upon completing the Dickens volumes, began what he saw as his final major project, a three-volume *Life* of Swift. He had been collecting materials for this project for more than twenty years; in fact, the eighteen boxes of Swiftiana now in the Forster Collection at the Victoria and Albert Museum still constitute the "preeminent assemblage of autographs and early printed books for the study of Swift."[71] The first volume of the *Swift* appeared at the end of 1875. It was widely reviewed (Forster clipped over 100 columns of newspaper and journal notices) and approved. There would be no more volumes published, however; indeed, there would be no more work of any kind from Forster's pen. He died suddenly on February 1, 1876. At the time of his death, Forster's wife was his only living relative, ten of the fifteen persons named in the playbills for the amateur theatricals for the Guild of Literature and Art were dead, and of the group gathered in Forster's chambers to hear the famous reading of *The Chimes* in 1844, only Carlyle was still alive.[72]

Forster was buried February 6, 1876, at Kensal Green Cemetery in the same tomb as his sister Elizabeth. His massive personal library resides as the Forster Collection in the Victoria and Albert Museum. This wonderful holding includes over 18,000 bound volumes, numerous paintings, sketches, and prints, autographs, and manuscripts reflecting his lifelong devotion to the history and literature of the seventeenth, eighteenth, and nineteenth centuries.

A most fitting and touching conclusion to this brief sketch of so full a life is afforded by the words on Forster's gravestone:[73]

In Memory of
JOHN FORSTER, ESQ.,
Historian, Biographer and Critic

———

Noted in private life
For the robustness of his character
And the warmth of his affections.
For his ceaseless industry in literature and business
And the lavish services in the midst of his crowded life
He rendered to friends;
For his keen appreciation of every species of excellence,
And the generosity of his judgments
On books and men.

———

Born 2nd April, 1812,
Died 1st February, 1876.

Chapter Two
Critic and Journalist
"Authors by Profession"

From the time the teenaged John Forster wrote the neighbor boy's mother that drama served "as a reinforcement of religion and the laws" until his death at sixty-four, Forster, as critic, editor, and biographer, extolled the moral and social values of literature, describing and eloquently defending the rights and virtues of "authors by profession."[1] As subeditor of the *Examiner* in charge of its literary and drama columns, Forster became to authors, publishers, and theater managers "perhaps the one most influential critic of the metropolitan press," increasing the stature and popularity of the *Examiner* by noticing "immediately on its appearance every work of the slightest merit, by converting what in other newspapers were puffs into criticisms careful and scholarly, and by heartiness of praise where praise was felt to be due."[2] His individual reviews reveal his specific critical theories, but these in turn can best be understood in the context of his unrelenting advocacy of the rights and dignities owed professional authors, an advocacy repeatedly expressed not only *en passant* but in articles explicitly devoted to these subjects.

Forster's support of professional writers can be traced to his relations with Leigh Hunt and Charles Lamb during his apprenticeship years in London, 1828–1833, when he established his journalistic credentials in the *New Monthly Magazine,* the *Athenaeum,* the *Courier,* and the *True Sun,* where he became chief drama critic. Hunt and Lamb proved valuable mentors to the young man: they opened important publishing channels to him, introduced him to the intentions and accomplishments of the chief English authors of the sixteenth, seventeenth, and eighteenth centuries, and helped him to develop critical precepts he would hold throughout his career.[3]

Each attracted the younger man as a professional author, albeit in somewhat different ways, and won him to dedicate himself to writing and the study of literature. Hunt affected most substantially Forster's critical appreciation of Shakespeare, eighteenth-century writers, and the potential of the stage. On his side, Forster admired Hunt as the accomplished poet and critic, essentially innocent of wrongdoing, who nevertheless had come to be misunderstood by many and whose work had fallen into disfavor. Forster moved to set right such error, and for nearly thirty years he took every available occasion to notice Hunt's publications, favorably reviewing his works, and to act behind the scenes with friends, publishers, and theater managers; finally, Forster helped secure a government pension for his earliest mentor.

Lamb, whose influence is most conspicuous in Forster's Shakespeare criticism, had none of Hunt's handicaps and represented the epitome of the man-of-letters. To Forster, Lamb's writing displayed a "delicate and extreme . . . sense of all that is human" equaled by "no one of the great family of authors past or present."[4] As a critic, Lamb was simply peerless: "Search English literature through, from its first beginnings till now, and you will find none like him. There is not a criticism he ever wrote that does not directly tell you a number of things you had no previous notion of. . . . In that very domain of literature with which you fancied yourself most variously and closely acquainted, he would show you 'fresh fields and pastures new,' and these the most fruitful and delightful . . . more valuable . . . when found, that they had eluded the search of ordinary men."[5] Throughout his career, Forster looked to Lamb as his critical model, and he cited Lamb more than any other authority in his *Examiner* columns. Indeed, Forster's personal ambition "to estimate and control the progress of the national literature"[6] dates from 1834, the time of Lamb's death and the year Forster's authoritative voice found its most powerful outlet in the *Examiner*.

Rights and Status for Authors

Convinced of literature's crucial role in society, Forster periodically devoted his *Examiner* columns to discussions of the rights and dignities due professional authors. An early major instance involved Serjeant Thomas Noon Talfourd's efforts in 1837 to change the British copyright laws, which then offered virtually no protection against piracy and expired at the author's death. Talfourd's bill called for copyright protection for sixty years. While the bill failed, the copyright controversy continued, and in a supportive article in 1839, Forster struck out sharply against opponents of a strengthened copyright law.

The tone as well as the substance and range of Forster's remarks constituted a powerful rebuttal of those who urged cheapness in the public's interest. Forster provided generous extracts from Talfourd's statements supporting the bill, employed effective name-dropping by mentioning the petitions of Wordsworth and Southey, and quoted at length from the petitions of Carlyle and Landor. He turned inside out the opposition's definition of "cheapness" by arguing: "The dearest book a man can possibly buy is a good for nothing one. It causes him to waste his money and time, only to injure his taste, understanding, and feeling—which he ought to regard beyond all price."[7] Forster was enraged that a group of mechanics who assembled books had filed a petition against the bill. He heaped ridicule upon them:

Why, the fable of the belly and the members is nothing to this fact: this is the wild rebellion of hands, legs, shoulders, coats, hats, breeches, shoes, beef, blacking, soap, and plum-pudding, aided and abetted by the "genius" of locomotion, against the very head and brain of mankind! Surely the great amount of intelligence which is well known to exist among the entire body of the mechanics, is attempted to be brought into very equivocal repute by this fraction of them who assume such superiority over the rest—and over all literature—by the showing of their petition![8]

In a calmer vein he concluded by praising the public's ability to look after itself, denying that the public was "a most feeble, helpless, and dull-eyed monster"; rather it could "very clearly distinguish between the interests of 'literature,' and the interests of 'printing'; between the diffusion of 'knowledge' and the diffusion of 'paper.' "[9]

In 1842, Forster returned briefly to the subject of copyright, this time international copyright, providing space in the *Examiner* for a circular by Dickens in which the novelist described efforts, particularly by American newspaper editors who reprinted popular British works, to forestall any change in the laws that might initiate international protection. Dickens exhorted all authors to avoid dealings with such editors and publishers and himself vowed to avoid entering into "any negotiation with any person for the transmission, across the Atlantic, of early proofs of anything I may write, and that I will forego all profit derivable from such a source."[10]

For the remainder of his career in journalism—to 1856—Forster let slip by no opportunity to argue on behalf of those who struggled honorably to earn a livelihood with their pens. A case in point is the notice accorded Laman Blanchard's *Sketches from Life* (1846), published shortly after the author's suicide and including a lengthy memoir of Blanchard by Bulwer. Forster opened his notice: "The life of a poor man of letters must be full of interest, if truly told."[11] The tone suggested by this opening is sustained throughout as Forster quotes extensively from Bulwer's generous memoir, detailing the struggles in journalism of the man they both had known for years on such periodicals as the *New Monthly Magazine,* the *Courier,* the *True Sun,* and the *Examiner.* Both men emphasized the stress and time-consuming labor of providing for a wife and four children via the fruits of newspaper journalism:

> There is *no* life in the world . . . not even that of the farm labourer, straining his sinews for seven or eight shillings weekly, to feed his family and pay his rent, that is so replete with all the varieties of misery as the life of the friendless man of letters, without a fixed engagement or a commanding name.
> For the lawyer there are many roads open to preferment; for the divine many; for the doctor some. The soldier and sailor may have pensions in the distant prospect. Even the citizen has his gown, his dinners, and the civic chair. But the literary man is *unplaced.* His position in society lies in that vast unsurveyed region called NOWHERE, in which so many of her Majesty's poorer lieges live, and breathe, and suffer, and run a long course, and die.[12]

Forster produced his most ambitious journalistic defense of the profession of literature in three *Examiner* articles that appeared in January 1850 and July 1851. The impetus for these essays was an article in the *Morning Chronicle* opposing all state patronage of letters, a piece that had itself grown out of a scene in Thackeray's *Pendennis* that concludes: ". . . it may be whispered *to those uninitiated people who are anxious to know the habits and make the acquaintance of men of letters, that there are no race of people who talk about books, or, perhaps, who read books, so little as literary men.*[13]

In his first response, Forster passed off Thackeray's remark as "caricature," though not without chastising the novelist for paying "court to the non-literary class by disparaging his literary fellow-labourers."[14] But Forster refused to dismiss so casually the *Chronicle's* major points, which were to him anathema: that "Protection to Literature or Science is mischievous in nearly the same way as protection to commerce"; that those writers with pensions were "literary paupers on the State"; that "Great Britain is already overstocked with authors of the middling and lower order . . . ; and [that] the love of notoriety inherent in mankind, combined with the common distaste for continuous or unexciting labour, will always attract an undue number of recruits from other employments to literature. There may be no harm in this, so long as they can pay their way. . . . But why swell the stream, or accelerate its flow, by State bounties?"[15]

Forster attacked such views as illogical and tasteless. No possible analogy can be asserted between the protection of commerce and that of literature or science. Nor are men accomplished in these fields paupers dependent on the State: "Services done to the State by distinguished efforts in art, literature, and science, are as un-equivocal, and at the least as important, as services done by professors of arms, law, divinity, and diplomacy. The claims of literature and science are for a due recognition and recompense of such valuable service rendered to the State. They are advanced, not in behalf of individuals, but of the class. They are not beggars' petitions, but demands for justice."[16]

Forster again took up the subject of the distinction justly due men of letters two weeks later, principally because in the intervening week, Thackeray, in an open letter to the *Chronicle,* objected to being accused of disparaging his calling or of any other base inten-tions. Thackeray's letter was the opening Forster needed. For several years he had been frustrated by the novelist's sarcastic portraits and open ridicule of his contemporary fellow authors, especially in his series of "*Punch's* Prize Novelists," which had lampooned both Bul-wer and Forster himself. Forster had elsewhere criticized Thackeray for his use of satire and contempt; he seized the current opportunity once again to lash out. He dismissed Thackeray's protest that the excerpt from *Pendennis* merely exposed the "vices and weaknesses notorious in certain members" of the writing profession. The fact remains, Forster asserted, that the "habits and manners of the 'men of letters' " Thackeray has exhibited are the "talk of a set of drunk-ards, rogues, and fribbles." Forster claimed that at the end of the controversial passage in the novel, Thackeray, in his own voice, directed his comments "without limit to all literary men"; since in the novel that comment is left "unexplained," Forster asked, "what would be its meaning but that the conversation and pursuits of men of letters are the reverse of intelligent, and that the non-literary may abate its curiosity respecting them?"[17]

Having dispensed with Thackeray for the time being, Forster moved to his principal concern, which was not so much the dignity of literature, per se, as the proper recognition due from the State for the "claims and services" of literature. Forster did not particularly admire the existing "system" of pensioning writers, but he wanted no deletion of such aid where it existed without a substitute plan already in place for providing financial assistance. He denounced the kind of thinking that could give Southey a baronetcy but no salary, and allow Godwin £70 a year for sweeping the Court of Exchequer, or, earlier, make Newton Master of the Mint and Burns an exciseman—positions for which the two men were incompetent and wherein they were destined to fulfill the predictions of many detractors. Speaking of Burns and Newton, Forster concluded: "To reward a poet or a philosopher by making him a diplomatist or a financier, is to run the risk of having the business of the State mismanaged, with the certainty of arresting useful and noble avocations which were enlarging social enjoyment and contributing to public happiness. It is bad economy to save a pension that might enable the student to pursue inquiries free from privation and care, by paying probably a larger stipend for having the State-business bungled."[18]

Returning to this issue in July 1851 in an article entitled "Ill-Requited Services," Forster summed up all he had been saying for the preceding twelve years about the rights, values, and appropriate status of professional men of letters. Again Thackeray had provided the impetus for Forster's comments. Finishing his last lecture on the English humorists, Thackeray alluded to the question of whether literature and men of letters were neglected, and concluded, "No, no, no." He asserted, "We do meet with kindness." Forster rejoined: but do "we meet with justice also? . . . . In all other states of Europe . . . literature and science cultivated with success are passports to public honours. The man who with a pen can influence opinion, or add to human knowledge . . . stands far before the man of the sword as a benefactor to his race. His intellect declares him qualified to think for his country, and it is by thought henceforward, not by force, that countries must be governed."[19]

Forster placed the higher class of men of letters above many lawyers and all of the nation's soldiers as thinkers whose contributions are invaluable to the State. But Forster called attention to the "pitiful disadvantage . . . the salaries of men of literature or science, when they happen to be officially employed," bear to those of "official doorkeepers, porters, and deliverers of parliamentary votes." The salary "tapers finely off," he noted, as the position "approaches the departments of thought or invention."[20]

In his conclusion, Forster continued to stress financial remuneration for authors as thinkers but returned to a consideration of their literary work and the issue of copyright. He did so by drawing an effective analogy to the birthright distinction accorded to succeeding generations by a government grateful for some wartime act of violence, "one man's worthless deed, which in strict justice would have merited the brand of scorn." Forster asserted: "Yet forsooth he is a visionary who would hint the possibility of preserving for the descendants of the truly great any part of the fortune which their forefathers created; though it is not with them even a question of preserving that which has been given from without. The destroyers may keep the hire of their destructiveness, and let it be paid on to their children for ever; but the creators may not keep even the smallest fraction of their own creation."[21]

Of the continental countries the shortest copyright guarantee at this time was twenty-five years in Russia, and in most countries it was perpetual. But England extended protection for a mere seven years. Forster argued that "the commonest dictates of natural justice require that at the least the widow and children of an author should not be beggared of their inheritance. . . ." And he concluded with the rhetorical question: "Are we not justified, with such facts and considerations before us, in refusing to admit that literature and science have yet obtained their due position in this country?"[22]

General Critical Theory

Doubtless, the writer on the *Critic* spoke truly in asserting that Forster set out "to estimate and to control the progress of the national literature." Necessarily, so weighty a mission could not be undertaken lightly, and Forster's serious and lifelong commitment manifested itself throughout the pages of his reviews, particularly in his assured and authoritative tone. Forster's judgments covered the full range of this "national literature," but generally, and most important, he evaluated the principal types: poetry, fiction, drama, history, and biography. Within understandable limits, he believed them possessed of similar functions and held them to essentially the same critical standards. Potentially, to Forster, each exerts a force for moral or social good. Instructing historians against a simplistic view of their subject, for example, Forster insisted that literature has an impact upon a nation's affairs that historians must consider: "It is a great mistake to suppose that strict matters of statesmanship are the only matters with which history has to do. In the present state of society more especially, it should be one of her first duties to trace the influence of literature and literary advancement . . . upon the action of politics, and to exhibit the latter, in its turn, influencing the national manners."[23] The critic who believes that literature can move a people in this way will naturally consider that books may have a pernicious as well as a salutary influence, and he will pursue his task as critic with a consummate seriousness. This was Forster's attitude, but it did not turn him into a snarling guard-dog, always on watch and ready to pounce. Forster espoused an essentially liberal philosophy, and the enormous range of his interests and his utter disdain for critics whose major function seemed to him to be faultfinding predisposed him to seek to appreciate and to enjoy what he reviewed.

Following Lamb's example, Forster labored where possible to be a discoverer in his criticism, opening up "fresh fields and pastures new" so that the full potential of a work to teach and delight its readers could be realized. His most consistent criteria were threefold, and included an insistence that the work (1) be true (i.e., faithful to reality); (2) provide a humane perspective on fundamental human passions and experiences; and (3) have a form so exactly embodying a unified concept and purpose as to produce a single effect or emotion. While these three criteria—realism, optimism, and unity— provided the tests Forster employed, final assessment usually rested on his judgment of what he called the "spirit of the book," a phrase incorporating a complex of elements—reaching out to include the "spirit" of the author. Two sentences in a review of Landor's *Imaginary Conversations* written in 1853 near the end of Forster's career as a critic encapsulate his general views (and anticipate by almost half a century the principles promulgated in Pater's famous essay on "Style"): "A book that *is* a book, no simulacrum, but a living mass of thoughts and feelings grouped in their particular way, made visible under their own peculiar form, cannot be characterised in a sentence. The spirit of such a book, in its lights and shades and wonderful varieties, not only resembles, but it really is—the spirit of a man."[24]

The three principal criteria constituted the heart of what was, in fact, a very generous critical philosophy. Of course, many works were found wanting: they failed in realism (Forster could be savage when he found cant, false emotion, and what he called "conventional absurdities" or "stale evasions"); they did not address fundamental human situations and emotions in a way calculated to encourage or to improve us; they lacked unity, perhaps because they reflected a hopeless mismatch of purpose and details, or perhaps the author's initial intention was lost, obscured, or abandoned. Nevertheless, in application Forster's philosophy was generous because it incorporated the Victorian humanist's point of view, to borrow from Browning, that "a man's reach" may "exceed his grasp" and that a man is the spirit he works in: not wholly what he does, or has done at a given point, but what he can and may do. In seeking to define the man in his work, Forster, unlike those critics who concentrated on faultfinding, often commended promise, gave encouragement, and predicted future success. If Forster found the work predominantly realistic and if it sympathetically rendered the universals of human experience and was informed by a unified vision adequately rendered in the main, he would downplay, but always remark, mere lapses in the parts. Like Ruskin in his essay on the Gothic, what counted most for Forster was the quality of the artist's imaginative vision, not minor inadequacies in technique. Using the Victorian doctrine of the imperfect, Forster could judge favorably the early works of Tennyson, Browning, and Dickens, and indeed some of their later works as well as those of Bulwer, Landor, and Carlyle, because, despite clear weaknesses in execution, the imaginations behind the works were clear-sighted, morally encouraging, and able to express themselves in coherent, reflective forms.

Forster sought no restrictions on subject matter for literature so long as the ugly or reprehensible in human affairs was not made attractive but rather used to show more clearly the benefits of the moral or ethical life. He frequently cited Fielding as an artist who worked in this manner. When glorification of crime became an issue in the Newgate fiction of Ainsworth, Bulwer, and Dickens, Forster sharply denounced novels like Ainsworth's *Jack Sheppard* but found praiseworthy those by Bulwer and Dickens, such as *Eugene Aram* and *Oliver Twist,* which presented similar materials while not portraying sympathetically criminals or criminal acts. He could and did speak out against rigid morality that would forbid literature to present any actions that were not conventionally approved, asking, "Are we to reduce everything to the level of our own morality?"[25] When some objected to Bulwer's *The Lady of Lyons,* Forster wondered whether they preferred to "reform the stage upon the plan of Jeremy Collier, and make it an echo of the pulpit instead of a reflection of the manners or the higher thoughts of the world."[26] Yet though his general moral position is more liberal than that of many of his contemporaries and though he opposed overt didacticism as a violation of art, Forster was consciously and deliberately a middle-class Victorian.[27]

Critic of Poetry

Forster consistently proclaimed the importance of poetry and sought to discover and popularize poetic genius. He believed of "true poetry" that nothing "is so well adapted for a popular circulation" because the poet "addresses himself to no section of mankind, but to humanity itself" for the purpose of "instruction and delight."[28] Forster felt that the moral and social potential of poetry is enormous in that the poet possesses the power to lift man to a sphere where he can "survey all things and consider their relative value, and learn to know whether they belong to the province of falsehood or truth."[29] Nevertheless poets of true genius, who have the deepest human truths to communicate, need most to fear that disruption of unity in a work's overall emotional impression which results from yielding to the didactic impulse. Wordsworth, whom Forster acclaimed "the greatest poet of this age,"[30] drew criticism occasionally on this account. Shelley, another admitted genius, was charged with the "great error" of making "his poetry too much a vehicle for his opinions," of not allowing "the poetic furor to have its way."[31] Shelley occasionally violated another of Forster's criteria: ". . . we rarely encounter realities—ordinary human passions—familiar thoughts—household phrases. . . ."[32]

The best way to appreciate and to assess Forster as a critic of poetry is to consider his evaluations over the more than two decades of his reviewing career—watching him apply his criteria specifically to writers whose works we, nearly 150 years later, know and value. His assessments of Browning and Tennyson suggest themselves for a variety of reasons: he first reviewed both men when they were unknown to him; he reviewed both men from the outset of their careers to the point where they reached the height of their artistic powers; his reviews had a perceptible effect on their reputations; his reviews, particularly of Browning, show the kind of balance that disproves the charge that he frequently merely "puffed" his friends; these reviews demonstrate the typical strengths and weaknesses of his critical work.

Browning's poetry published during Forster's reviewing years provides ample opportunities to demonstrate the generosity of Forster's critical philosophy and the willingness he showed to extenuate when in the presence of poetic genius. Equally obvious is his ability to recognize on his own the existence and promise of such genius. He came to *Paracelsus* in September 1835 within three weeks of the poem's publication having no knowledge of Browning and guessing that this poem was his first publication. (*Pauline*, 1833, appeared without the author's name and was soon withdrawn due to poor sales.)

The poem elicited from the critic almost unqualified praise. Despite certain difficulties the reader encounters in *Paracelsus*, Forster found that it exhibits a "rich vein of internal sentiment, a deep knowledge of humanity, an intellect subtle and inquisitive . . . unequivocal power" and beauty enough "to compensate" the reader for the "tedious passages, were they ten times as obscure and tedious." Forster read the book twice and suggested that the reader would probably enjoy doing the same, and he predicted a "brilliant career" for the poet "if he continues true to the present promise of his genius."[33]

Within six months, Forster again applauded *Paracelsus*, using Browning and the poem as the subject for the first section of a three-part series of articles in the *New Monthly Magazine* detailing his discovery of "Evidences of a New Genius for Dramatic Poetry." Forster and Browning had developed a close friendship by this time, but in his nineteen-page essay, Forster was all serious business. As in the *Examiner* review, Forster's critical criteria provided the central test: the poem is true or faithful to reality, and it deals with fundamental human issues with sympathy and understanding: ". . . it embraces . . . so many of the highest questions, and glances with such masterly perception at some of the deepest problems, of man's existence . . . that they open up on every side of us in the

actual world, new sources of understanding and sympathy."[34] The
poem is not didactic: no idea, as such, is forced on the reader.
Rather, the power of the piece derives from its dramatic presentation
of mood and psychology of character: "Passion is invariably displayed, and never merely analysed." The coherence of the vision is
never undermined. Browning has the power of a "great dramatic
poet; we never think of Mr. Browning while we read his poem; we
are not identified with him, but with the persons into whom he
has flung his genius." In this, Browning passes the highest and
"essential dramatic test" and "is never found wanting": *"In the
agitation of the feelings, sight is given to the imagination."*[35]

Browning's drama *Strafford,* produced at Covent Garden on May
1, 1837, challenged both Forster's skill and his integrity as a critic:
he had written, with Browning's help as we have seen, a biography
of Strafford, a work that Browning noted favorably in the preface
to his play; he had encouraged Browning to write for the stage,
seeing the poet's greatest strengths in dramatic presentation of character; he had helped preserve the mutual friendship among Macready, Browning, and himself despite frequent quarreling during
production preparation and last-minute rewriting. The review is
typical of those Forster wrote for Browning, reflecting a balance of
praise and blame, finally tipped in favor of the poet's genius in spite
of obvious flaws in execution.

The production itself, Forster felt, was unremarkable and would
not "take permanent hold of the stage." Confining himself principally to the written work, he found fault with a sometimes weak
plot but alleged as the most serious defect a blurring of the tragic
implications of the story through an inappropriate concentration on
the personal and domestic side of Strafford's character. The audience
was denied "the pity and terror which might have been made to
impend over his scaffold . . . the awful lesson of a Nation's Retribution."[36] Nevertheless, as a poet seeking to make real the characters
delineated, Browning was again faultless: ". . . we will now say
that a more thoroughly dramatic style than that in which Mr.
Browning has worked out his own conception of Strafford could not
possibly be conceived." And he concluded: *"Strafford* suggests the
most brilliant career of dramatic authorship that has been known
in our time."[37]

Forster did not review *Sordello* (1840). The critics who did "re-
sponded as with one voice, burying *Sordello* under a heap of epi-

thets—'obscure,' 'trash of the worst description,' 'unread-able.' . . ."[38] While as a result of *Sordello*'s failure other reviewers noted Browning less often, Forster reviewed each of the eight works in the series entitled *Bells and Pomegranates* (1841–1846), and, in general, his judgments chart Browning's slow-paced discovery of what was, in Forster's opinion, the poet's proper métier. We can track in a brief survey Forster's critical reaction, one that despite continued praise often reveals the critic's frustration over Browning's obscurity, metaphysics, and "harsh" verses.

Reviewing *Pippa Passes* (1841), which he strongly approved, Forster recapitulated Browning's career, putting even *Sordello* in a more favorable light: "To write a bad poem is one thing," but "to write a poem on a bad system is another, and very different." When critics come to *Sordello* hereafter, he predicted, "it will not be admired for its faults, but in spite of them, its power and its beauty will be perceived. It had a magnificent aim, and a great many passages in which justice was done to that and to the genius of the designer."[39]

Excepting the scene between the young sculptor and his bride, Forster accorded *Pippa Passes* the highest praise: it is "worthy of the writer of *Paracelsus*. We call it, without doubt, a piece of right inspiration. It is in a dramatic form, and has fine dramatic transitions, but its highest beauty is lyrical."[40] *The Tragedy of King Victor and King Charles* (1842) is a flawed drama principally "in its substitution of the metaphysics of character and passion for their broad and practical results."[41] *Dramatic Lyrics,* however, Forster held to show that Browning was mastering his proper form (Forster's was virtually the only critical notice of this publication): "in the simple and manly strain of some of these *Dramatic Lyrics,* we find proof of the firmer march and steadier control. Mr. Browning will win his laurel."[42] Forster believed that *A Blot in the 'Scutcheon* (1843) as a stage production would not long appeal and was weakened in not having much to "touch humanity"; yet "we would give little for the feelings of the man who could read this tragedy without a deep emotion." The play had no faults that demanded exposure and had to the good a just morality, "animated pathos," and "freshness and unexaggerated strength."[43]

Forster struggled to approve *Colombe's Birthday* (1844), the last drama Browning wrote for the stage. He observed that this "play gives sterling proof of Mr. Browning's genius," and has both "passion" and "thought." But its material lacked broad appeal. Forster's

conclusion was direct and more forthright than normal: "As far as
he has gone, we abominate his tastes as much as we respect his
genius."[44] Within a year, however, Forster was jubilant over *Dramatic Romances and Lyrics* (1845), for Browning had found his way:
"Our readers know how high we have ranked his muse; and how
we have grieved when she lost her way in transcendental or other
fogs and, like poor Origen's fallen star, 'rayed out' only darkness.
Here she has found the path again."[45]

The final two reviews of Browning show Forster confident in his
praise and feeling justified that he had been correct all along in his
assessment of Browning as an original genius. Forster devoted six
columns to *Christmas-Eve and Easter-Day* (1850); except for some
qualms over what he termed Browning's religious dogmatism—
"not a few passages" constitute "but another form of a common
bigotry"—he bestowed unqualified praise following the lines of his
specific critical canons—reality, concern with human problems in
a humane spirit, and an artistically satisfying whole:

He is equally a master of thought and emotion, and joins to a rare power
of imaginative creation that which is still more rarely found in union with
it—the subtlest power of mental reasoning and analysis. Over the instrument of language he exerts the most facile mastery, and few poets have
moved with such free and flowing step through the most complicated
word-mazes of music and measure. . . . The feeling of this poem is true,
whatever may be thought of its dogmatism; and its essential teaching is
independent of particular forms. It will assuredly waken very many to the
'better part' suggested by its theme, and it will stir and quicken thought
in all.[46]

Forster's review of *Men and Women* (1855) was his last of Browning
before leaving the *Examiner*. Its praise reflected Forster's pride in
having early discovered a poetical genius and having shepherded
him for twenty years through trial and error, good times and bad.
He again pointed out problems of obscurity and harsh measures,
Browning's "old fault" that he and most reviewers had often criticized, but in his concluding remarks he obviously intended to
weaken such objections: "Since his first poem was published twenty
years ago, when we were the first to promise him the reputation he
has won, this journal has been incessantly objecting to it [obscurity]." Now Forster worried that such criticism could be carried too
far:

. . . the perceptions of a poet, when applied to thoughts of more than common subtlety, will often necessarily outrun his reader's. Such obscurity proceeds from fullness, not emptiness; and it is not always that a thought which is hard to follow will be found not worth the exercise of mind required for overtaking it. A distinctive quaintness, a complete absence of diffuseness, and the inborn dramatic feeling which is often apt to suggest breaks of phrase, and striking interruptions to a train of thought, are among the chief causes of what is most complained of in Mr. Browning. They are part of the writer's individuality. . . .[47]

And it is by virtue of his individuality that Browning will live for posterity, if he is to live at all, Forster concludes. He does not mean to ignore flaws in certain poems, but the overwhelming truth and the point for final emphasis is that much in *Men and Women* is as "genuine as poetry as any that has been written in our time."[48]

By and large, Forster's reviews of Browning's works were a credit to the critic. Very clear in these assessments is his desire to identify the poet's purpose and to understand, elucidate, and laud what was praiseworthy despite what he saw as flaws in technique and, occasionally, in subject matter. The critiques are not mere "puffs"; they represent the mind of a liberal critic, confident in his discovery of poetic genius, praising and blaming but consistently encouraging the "fine tuning" of that genius.

If Browning sometimes seemed to dare Forster to praise the poet's genius, Tennyson presented the critic few such problems. From the earliest notice of Tennyson's work, that of *Poems* in 1833, through his last published criticism of the then Poet Laureate, that of *Maud and Other Poems* in 1855, Forster described a virtually continuous rise in the poet's artistic control and critical reputation.

When *Poems* appeared at the end of 1832, Forster was writing for the *True Sun,* where in January 1833 he recorded his first estimate of Tennyson's work. He accorded him recognition as a "true poet" whose position hereafter would be "the most high, if his maturity answer to the promise of his youth." The review follows the points in Forster's critical canon: Tennyson has "the true spirit of poetry" and "words fit to enshrine it"; he has feeling in its "widest range," "delicacy," a "fervid sympathy," and "imagination at will." Forster concluded: "We could point to no living poet, with such a luxuriously intense feeling of beauty. . . ." There were, indeed, weaknesses, principally excess of imagery and some liberty with rhyme. Yet, by and large, the review offered unqualified praise and singled

out particular poems for special notice. "The Miller's Daughter" is
a typical example: "exquisite throughout—full of the calm beauty
of contented happiness, reflecting back a youthful passion—of heart-
affection—of simplicity and homely truth."[49]

When *Poems* in two volumes appeared in 1842, Forster immediately reviewed them, noting the advances in Tennyson's technique.
Tennyson has mastered "selection and compression." His concept
of the "beautiful . . . has become more chastened, more intellectual, less alloyed." His descriptions "have a sharper and more def-
inite outline"; his verse is "stronger and more varied." Forster's
concluding exhortation urged the poet to advance even further: "In
a word, we think that he would find himself able to fly a higher
flight than lyric, idyl, or eclogue, and we counsel him to try it."
His comments on "Locksley Hall," which Forster predicted would
be the favorite of the volumes, show the critic's preferences: ". . .
a piece of strong, full-blooded, man's writing. . . . It is full of
daring conception, and most bitter passion, and the verse rushes on
with a wild solemn flow, in splendid unison with the theme."[50]

The Princess (1848) justified Forster's continued confidence, although he felt that the poem was "irregular, even clumsy, in its
structure." His principal frustration centered upon Tennyson's choice
of form for his purpose: "He had something serious to say—why
graft it on burlesque? . . . Eminently in the manliness of his
thoughts, in the largeness of his view, and in his power of clothing
the familiar in our human passions and affections 'with golden
exhalations of the dawn,' he is worthy to be the poet of our time.
Why does he not assume his mission?"[51]

Indeed the promise of the 1842 volumes seemed to Forster not
fully realized until 1850, when his commendation of *In Memoriam*
included comparison with Dante, Petrarch, Shakespeare, and Mil-
ton. Again Forster's critical axioms provide the frame for his assessment. *In Memoriam* was grounded in the actual world; it dealt
with eternal human themes optimistically; its form conveyed its
generating impulse perfectly: "It is the record of a healthy and
vigorous mind working its way, through suffering, up to settled
equipoise and hopeful resignation. The effect of the poem, as a
whole, is to soften yet to strengthen the heart; while every separate
part is instinct with intense beauty, and with varied and profound
reflections on individual man, on society, and on their mutual
relations. It is perhaps the author's greatest achievement. A passion,

deep-felt throughout it, has informed his ever subtle thoughts and delicate imagery with a massive grandeur and a substantial interest."[52]

The passions of *Maud* differ radically from those informing *In Memoriam,* and Forster had been unequivocal in condemning such displays of passion in the works of the Spasmodic poets. Yet when he approached *Maud and Other Poems* (1855), the last review he wrote of Tennyson's work, he found the title piece unsurpassed for "pure description," "instinct with the subtlest perceptions," and "deep feeling and purpose," and suitable in form for its subject and theme: "a fine mind troubled by disease."[53] With regard to Tennyson, then, as with Browning, Forster could end his reviewing career in 1855 confident that a genius he had early recognized and encouraged had reached the height of his powers and that his poetry was appreciated by a wide audience in part recruited and prepared by the critic's loyal and constant notice in his *Examiner* columns.

Critic of Fiction

Forster evaluated fiction applying very much the same critical standards he used for poetry—realism, universal themes treated positively, and artistic coherence.[54] He looked to the eighteenth-century masters for his models—Defoe, Goldsmith, Smollett, and particularly Fielding. Defoe, for example, was the great realist of English fiction, whereas Fielding set the standards for plotting and characterization. On the crucial matter of tone, too, Forster cited Fielding: the novelist was positive; he communicated his purpose in each work—to convey to the reader a sense of man's potential for excellence—via a powerful, albeit entertaining, presentation of man and the world as they actually exist.

Forster opposed didacticism as a valid impulse for literary expression and condemned evidence of such motivation often. The function of the artist, he believed, was not to moralize but rather to afford a moral and optimistic perspective on human actions and relationships. This specific element of his critical philosophy caused him repeatedly to comment upon subject matter and tone in his reviews. Indeed, Forster most fully expressed his broad critical tenets respecting fiction when writing on these issues; he addressed them at length during two specific imbroglios: what is appropriate subject matter for fiction, during the controversy that developed around the Newgate fiction of the 1830s, which featured criminals as major characters? And, in an extension of the issue into another social milieu and onto more complex features of characterization, what is the proper authorial perspective or tone in novels of social satire, such as Dickens's or Thackeray's? Forster viewed treatment or technique as the primary artistic issue since it is through technique that the author's moral vision is conveyed:

> It is indeed never the subject that can be objectionable, if the treatment is not so. . . . Swindlers and thieves are our associates in *Gil Blas;* we shake hands with highwaymen and housebreakers all round in the *Beggars' Opera;* we pack cards with La Ruse or pick pockets with Jonathan in Fielding's *Mr. Wild the Great* . . . but our morals stand none the looser for any of them. . . . Familiar with the lowest kind of abasement of life, the knowledge is used . . . to teach what constitutes its essential elevation. . . . We cannot too often be told that, as the pride and grandeur of mere external circumstance is the falsest of earthly things, so the truth of virtue in the heart is the most lovely and lasting.[55]

Using such standards, Forster was able to exempt Dickens from the charge of immorality in the handling of criminals in *Oliver Twist,* to make extenuations for his friend Bulwer, and to savage a novel like William Harrison Ainsworth's *Jack Sheppard* for its pernicious handling of its subject. With Dickens *reality* is always foremost; he never blinks at the essentially depraved and repellent nature of vice and crime: "Few writers have achieved a nobler moral than that which is embodied here . . . and none with so little of distortion in the means, or of compromise in the end. Vice loses nothing of its grossness, and virtue nothing of her triumph. The bad are not allowed to whine or blubber themselves all at once into the privileges of the good. . . . Everything in short is as we see it in life, and the retribution or repentance—the one too late, the other perhaps even too terrible—what we see there also."[56]

With Bulwer's criminal characters Forster was not always comfortable, but generally he accepted the novelist's intentions as worthy: in *Eugene Aram* he quibbled over historical accuracy; in *Paul Clifford* he conceded the value of the social and political satire; in *Lucretia,* he stepped forward in the face of charges of immorality leveled by other critics to defend the freedom of conscientious artists: "No man has a right to string together horrors gratuitously; but there is no horror, however appalling, supposing it affords an opportunity of examining the heart, and of tracing the relations of action to character and of character to action (the wisest lesson in morals, according to Swift), which the artist in fiction or the drama may not claim to use."[57]

With Ainsworth's *Jack Sheppard,* however, Forster found no defense possible due to the novelist's treatment of his hero, a notorious highwayman and murderer. Forster raged against the novel in an extraordinarily detailed review of nine columns, replete with long extracts of dialogue and description labeled "vile," "absurd," "disgusting," "incredible," and "immoral":

Soon . . . crime—bare, rascally, unmitigated, ferocious crime—becomes the idea constantly thrust before us. From that instant all of what with courtesy we will call the interest of the book may be said to hang upon the gallows. . . . The sentiments of the work are pretty constant to two great principles . . . a slavish adulation of high birth . . . and a strong sense of the moral capabilities, nice emotions, and sensitive affections, which belong to thieves and murderers. . . . We again say that we regret the necessity which forces us to this plain speaking.[58]

Another major provocation for Forster to expatiate upon questions of subject matter and treatment in fiction occurred in the late 1840s. The issues had broadened from presentation of criminals in Newgate fiction to consideration of social comment in the sweeping canvases of Dickens and Thackeray. Again Forster looked to Fielding as the premier exemplum of the social satirist. Dickens satisfied Forster's critical requisites: an essentially moral and optimistic perspective is offered on a series of significant human experiences described in a form appropriate to the author's purpose and producing his intended effect. Thackeray, on the other hand, is found wanting—in *Vanity Fair, Pendennis,* and *Henry Esmond* (1848–1852). Forster believed that Thackeray's principal artistic weakness was authorial perspective or tone, resulting in a depiction of society false or distorted, and a world view unpleasant where it was not offensive.

In reviewing *Vanity Fair,* Forster saw Thackeray in a position similar to Fielding's when he set about satirizing conventional morality by parodying Richardson's *Pamela.* But Fielding possessed a "genial cordiality" not found in Thackeray, and he very early moved beyond his intended joke: "The manly character of his hero, the sublime *bonhomie* of Parson Adams, the ripe beauty and exquisite goodness of Fanny, became a thousand times more congenial to him than mere burlesque or sneering ever could. . . ." Thackeray's

satire on conventional mores pales before Fielding's because no equal
amount of "large cordiality" has raised him "entirely above the
region of the sneering, into that of simple uncontaminated human
affection." Forster calls *Vanity Fair* "Rascality Fair," a much "less
true view of society than Fielding's."[59]

Forster believed that *Vanity Fair*'s weaknesses grow out of characterization. Individually, the characters are credible, but the "at-
mosphere of the work is overloaded with . . . exhalations of human
folly and wickedness. We gasp for a more liberal alternation of
refreshing breezes of unsophisticated honesty. . . . [The] moral is
insisted upon . . . and illustrations of it are heaped upon us with
a redundant profusion, unalleviated by a sufficient amount of more
gratifying images, that seems to us to go beyond the limits of the
pleasurable, and consequently of true art."[60]

Forster did not review *Pendennis* (1850), though he alleged in
private correspondence that its faults were those of *Vanity Fair,* but
he returned to similar objections in 1852, when reviewing *Henry
Esmond.* These comments reflect what we have so often seen before.
Thackeray fails because he does not "present pictures of life that we
can regard as true copies"; he does not "observe the world generously,
and with abundant sympathy, moving among the characters he
notices not as their judge but their companion, who would acquire
a delicate perception of those shades of opinion and feeling which
are found most commonly in combination with each other." Instead
we too often feel that "Mr. Thackeray is bending with a smile of
pity; turning up now and then the prettiest coat, to show some dirt
upon the lining, exhibiting to us something adorable, that he may
aggravate our perception in it of something detestable. . . ."[61]

Critic of Drama

Some of Forster's most memorable columns as well as some of
his least interesting appeared in the "Theatrical Examiner." From
1832 to about 1840, at first for the *True Sun* and then beginning
in 1834 for the *Examiner,* he wrote numerous reviews of new plays
and revivals. His best work includes the record of his reactions to
Shakespeare productions, to the works of such important contemporary dramatists as Sheridan Knowles, Edward Bulwer, and Robert
Browning, and to the major actors and actresses of his day—Edmund
and Charles Kean, William Charles Macready, Edwin Forrest, Rachel,

and Jenny Lind. The "Theatrical Examiner" columns, taken as a whole, are inferior to those of "The Literary Examiner," primarily because English drama did not possess talent in these years comparable to that of the other literary genres. Forster recognized and often bemoaned the dearth of dramatic genius, and he wrote fewer and fewer "Theatrical Examiner" columns in the last fifteen years of his reviewing, 1840 1855.[62] Undoubtedly, his most notable and interesting reviews are those analyzing Macready's performances of Shakespeare's tragedies and those comparing the acting styles of Macready and the American tragedian Edwin Forrest; these reviews live even today for their detailed and insightful analyses of the actors' performances and for the long interpretive passages of Shakespeare criticism Forster interpolated into his commentary.

Forster's criticism, especially of Shakespeare, shows a primary debt to Charles Lamb and Leigh Hunt. His Shakespeare criticism, indeed, shared both ideas and verbal echoes with that of Lamb. From Lamb, specifically, can be traced his desire to restore Shakespeare's original texts; and from Lamb, or from the general Romantic critical theory Lamb and Hunt shared with others, can be traced his emphasis on the organic form in the work and the importance of the psychological dimensions of character. From Hunt he absorbed a belief in the viability of the staged production and an emphasis on the human or ordinary side of the tragic hero's personality and actions, a "domestication" of tragedy.[63] On these very grounds, in fact, and using the same critical principles he repeatedly invoked respecting the purpose of literature, he convinced Macready to restore the character of the Fool in *King Lear,* after an absence from the stage for more than 150 years. In this particular instance, Forster believed that audiences would not sufficiently identify with Lear, whose suffering might seem "too frightful, a sublimity too remote, a grandeur too terrible"; the Fool's role, he argued, would bridge this distance "by quiet pathos . . . homely and familiar illustrations."[64]

Forster's influence as a drama critic equaled, if it did not surpass, the authority generally accorded his judgments on books. George Bernard Shaw, writing two decades after Forster's death, claimed that the "world's belief" that Macready was a better actor than Edwin Forrest was "not its own opinion, but Forster's." Comparing Forster with George Henry Lewes, the foremost English critic of the generation following Forster's, Shaw praised both men for possessing the critic's primary characteristic: "They could really and objectively see the stage; and they could analyze what they saw there. In this respect Forster is as good as Hazlitt or Lewes: he is a first-rate demonstrator, and can take an actor to pieces and put him together again as well as anybody."[65]

Forster would have appreciated such approval. He himself described the value to posterity of a critic's ability to allow readers to "see" the gifted actor performing the great role: "What would we give to have a minute record of Taylor's *Hamlet*, acted under the eye of SHAKESPEARE himself? What to have some remembrance of the imaginative sublimity of the *Ghost*, of the pathetic devotion of *Adam* in *As You Like It*, as those were doubtlessly expressed by SHAKESPEARE himself? They have perished utterly. Not so with the *Hamlet* and *Falstaff* of Betterton, the *Lear* and *Abel Drugger* of GARRICK. . . . All praise then to the critics of past days and of our own, the STEELES, CIBBERS, CUMBERLANDS, HUNTS, HAZLITTS, TALFOURDS, LAMBS."[66]

Forster demonstrated his ability to "take an actor to pieces," in the negative sense, in reviews of the American favorite Edwin Forrest. The actor was a rival to Macready, Forster's good friend; yet the extended analyses of Forrest's work make clear that Forster's damning criticism was consistent with his critical tenets. Forrest's principal weakness, a lack of imagination, was most clearly manifested in his tendency to overdramatize certain emotional states, particularly through excessive physical actions, and thereby to ignore, oversimplify, or otherwise "flatten" equally important emotional moods and to deny to major characters the psychological complexities of their personalities. Further, such emotions as were expressed often seemed disconnected, not clearly aspects of a single, multi-faceted personality: "We would say, generally, that there was a want of fusion in his acting. His passages of tenderness or rage are not struck out of each other. They are 'framed and glazed' by themselves. He wants that fine faculty of the imaginative in style which works a harmony with differents."[67]

King Lear provided Forster a case in point, showing how a fundamental misrepresentation of character could result from weaknesses such as Forrest's. Reviewing Forrest's portrayal of Lear in act 2, and after a lengthy exegesis of the state of Lear's mind, specifically in the storm scene, Forster leads up to Forrest's inept portrayal by explaining how the actor should approach the character of Lear so as to emphasize the grandeur of the man even amidst his suffering:

We would have him tighten and make rigid in those scenes every nerve of his frame, and elevate to its extremist point of elevation every burst of *Lear*'s wandering intellect. Nothing should be feebly given. Everything is here at its utmost point of tension. Yet what did Mr. Forrest? He entered upon the scene slowly, and recited the "Blow wind," etc. with a deliberate and stop-watch emphasis which reminded us of our exercises at the breaking up of school! . . . The same alternation of senseless tones was continued to the close of the tragedy. Wherever a remote point for the expression of physical misery occurred it was thrown out before everything else. We saw nothing before us but a "Foolish fond old man," whom we wanted, as Mr. Lamb has said, "to take into shelter and to relieve."[68]

In Macready's performances, particularly of Shakespeare's tragedies, Forster took great pleasure. Macready, he believed, captured in the spirit of his roles the playwright's intentions and, equally important, due to Forster's prodding, he returned to the stage the original texts. Over and over Forster lauds Macready in the roles of Shakespeare's major figures: Lear, Marc Antony, Iago, Hamlet, Macbeth. The reviews record Forster's minor quibbles—now with a cadence of speech, now with some stage business in a certain scene—but on the whole Macready is wonderfully apt in his characterizations, powerful in his effects, and successful in exactly those areas where Forrest was found wanting. Forster strives to make the reader "see":

. . . Mr. Macready, whose management of the murder itself [in *Othello*], and whose ghastly and tremendous appearance after it—suddenly starting with extended arms through the curtain that had been drawn over the deed—were in the highest possible taste and knowledge of his art, and in knowledge, too, of that characteristic of nature, which gives to the imagination a more terrible seeing than to the eye. We never saw a more complete effect—it was too fearful, if such an objection may be urged. We were startled indeed on the first night by a striking addition to its reality, for a woman in the pit had hysterically fainted. In the milder passages of agonised misery which occur towards the conclusion, Mr. Macready was equally great.[69]

As a final point regarding Forster's drama criticism, we should note how the addition of astute, if not always highly original,

interpretation of Shakespeare's texts enriches many of these reviews.
Two brief examples will indicate Forster's enthusiasm for and knowledge of Shakespeare, whom he would quote at length at the slightest
provocation.

Of Shylock:

. . . *Shylock* has a thousand things besides to express—humour, as well
as passion; wit, as well as reason. His intellect is supreme. His sense of
outraged justice is as quiet, deep and fervid as his purpose of revenge. He
meets his enemies with an honest vice, which is better than their hypocritical virtue. He brings things to a far more fitting level than the exclusive
Christians desired. In this it is evident Shakespeare meant to illustrate
something beyond revenge. He gives *Shylock,* in truth, the subtlest play
of intellect, the most intense fervour of eloquence and passion, the most
masterly elasticity and presence of mind—that in his person outraged
reason should be defended, insulted humanity practically vindicated, and
the tables turned on a set of cruel persecutors. . . .[70]

Of Othello:

The very awfulness and pitiless desolation of the catastrophe is a part of
the moral grandeur of this extraordinary play; and it is only when, through
all *Othello*'s fierce fluctuations of passion, the enduring impression left is
of the nobleness rather than the fierceness of his nature—when not sus-
picion but an offended sense of right is made the motive to his crime,
and the crime itself appears a sacrifice and not a murder—that we should
feel the actor has truly risen to the greatness of this wonderful character.[71]

Chapter Three

Historian and
Historical Biographer

Historian

John Forster withdrew from the *Examiner* and the burdens of journalism in January 1856 partly because his appointment as Secretary
to the Lunacy Commission afforded him a modest financial security.
As important in his decision, however, was the desire to pursue
that scholarship and writing he considered to be his most significant
work—historical studies of the English Commonwealth in the seventeenth century. Indeed, some of his first published writing when
a young man new to London had included sketches for *Englishman's
Magazine* of several of the principals in the parliamentary opposition
to Charles I during the period leading to the Civil Wars and the
Commonwealth.[1]

Forster made time for historical research and publication throughout his career, with his single greatest concentration of work coincident with the period 1836–1840, when, as subeditor and literary
critic for the *Examiner,* he was establishing himself in the London
press as a major voice on literature and drama. During these years,
he published for Dionysius Lardner's *Cabinet Cyclopaedia: Lives of
Eminent British Statesmen* five volumes of historical portraits of leading
figures in the struggle against Charles I: Sir John Eliot and Thomas
Wentworth (1836), John Hampden and John Pym (1837), Sir Henry
Vane and Henry Marten (1838), and Oliver Cromwell (2 vols. 1838–
39);[2] in 1840, these studies were collected into a single volume,
The Statesmen of the Commonwealth of England, to which Forster added
an introductory "Treatise on the Popular Progress in English History."[3] In 1845–46, he assisted his friend Douglas Jerrold in launching *Jerrold's Shilling Magazine,* publishing in the first four volumes
fourteen chapters of approximately fifteen pages each on the history
of the English monarchy from the time of the Norman conquest to
the reign of Henry III. In 1850–52, he edited anonymously in four

volumes the diary and letters of John Evelyn, providing extensive notes and an introduction.[4] "The Civil Wars and Oliver Cromwell," a lengthy review-essay in the *Edinburgh Review*, followed in 1856,[5] and in 1858 came the publication of two volumes of *Historical and Biographical Essays*, including "The Debates on the Grand Remonstrance," "The Plantagenets and the Tudors," and a reprinted and enlarged version of "The Civil Wars and Oliver Cromwell."[6] In 1860 appeared *Arrest of the Five Members by Charles the First* and a companion volume, *The Debates on the Grand Remonstrance, November and December, 1641,* and a slightly enlarged reprinting of two of the *Historical Essays* of 1858.[7] His greatest triumph of historical research followed in 1864, a two-volume biography of Sir John Eliot based on much unedited material then only recently discovered and made available to Forster by Eliot's descendants.[8]

Without doubt Forster overestimated the ultimate importance of his contributions to historical literature. Much that he wrote has been qualified by modern scholars; some of it, indeed, was seriously modified in his own time. Writing an obituary notice of Forster in the *Academy,* however, fellow historian Samuel Gardiner noted that it will be "an evil day for historical research" when the merits of men like Forster are no longer recognized. In an accurate and sympathetic final appraisal, observing that Forster never singled out for praise unworthy men or ideas, Gardiner concluded:

The merits and defects of his work sprang from the same source. He was an advocate, not a judge. He had sledge-hammer blows to deal against the mere semblance of history which passed muster before him, and he was too impatient of the nonsense which was talked by writers like the elder Disraeli to enquire whether some residuum of sense might not be found beneath it all. He was deficient in that judicious skepticism with which an historian is bound to test his assertions, and he therefore frequently, in spite of his love of hard work and his constant reference to original authorities, made assertions which will not bear the test of serious investigation.[9]

Forster's longtime friend Edward Bulwer offered a similar judgment in a fifty-page review article of *The Debates on the Grand Remonstrance* and of the *Arrest of the Five Members by Charles the First,* commending "the important additions he has made to our historical literature" but at the same time issuing a warning to the reader: "To much patience of research he unites a remarkable power of generalization, and he groups his details so as to render clear and prominent the facts he desires to enforce. . . . As his nature is hearty and his convictions deep, so his preferences cannot fail to be decided."[10] For Bulwer, whose political views were directly antithetical to the radical liberalism of Forster, these "decided convictions" led to some "warping" of the truth and caused Bulwer to "dissent from his conclusions."[11]

That Forster wrote as an advocate when presenting the issues is both understandable and undeniable. He was a trained lawyer. More to the point, such a charge would have pleased him, for he claimed the role of advocate in each of his works. In the introductory remarks to "A History for Young England," for example, he fumed against those contemporary historians who served the "coming generation" of young people as "influences fatal to sense and liberty" by evaluating crucial historical moments as follows: "The Revolution a Fraud. The Reformation a shabby Conspiracy. The houses of Legislature an impediment to the blessings of Monarchy. . . . "[12] Forster promised corrective history consisting of *"plain-speaking"* and, of course, the advocate's perspective: "I do not hold . . . that, to be a good historian, one should have no religion, no country, no profession, and no party. I have all of these; and would not willingly part with any" ("Young England," 85).

To appreciate Forster's tone and purpose, one must recognize two of his fundamental beliefs: (1) liberty can best be preserved by understanding the past, since the "Present can have no counsellor— the Future no protecting Angel—so sure and certain as the Past discloses";[13] and (2) the central historical event the people of England must properly understand and value is the Revolution against the tyranny of Charles I and the establishment of the Commonwealth. In his dedicatory note to the biography of Sir John Eliot, Forster eloquently expressed this idea: "TO ALL WHO VALUE THE REGULATED LIBERTY ENJOYED IN ENGLAND, WHO ATTRIBUTE ITS PRESERVATION TO A POWERFUL LEGISLATURE, AND WHO HAVE ANY INTEREST IN KNOWING WHAT WAS DONE AND SUFFERED TWO HUNDRED AND THIRTY YEARS AGO TO ESTABLISH THE INDEPENDENCE OF THE HOUSE OF COMMONS, I OFFER THIS ACCOUNT OF SIR JOHN ELIOT.[14]

In politics Forster was a Whig, and his view of history was that characteristic of his party. Indeed all of Forster's publications, whether biographical sketches, surveys covering hundreds of years of British monarchy, or in-depth analyses of specific issues and events, may be seen as explaining "the popular progress of English history," that is, the gradual winning over by "THE PEOPLE" of their individual freedoms and civil liberties beginning with the first Norman kings and culminating when an all-powerful House of Commons defied a tyrannical sovereign in the 1640s. Forster definitely wrote to place in proper perspective the struggles and achievements of the founders of the Commonwealth and saw in this purpose a distinct need for strong advocacy: ". . . the times, awful as they were, were not greater than the men. The ideas of both present themselves to us at once, like shadowy and solid giants standing together. . . . It is a grave reproach to English political biography, that the attention so richly due to the statesmen who opposed Charles I, in themselves the most remarkable men of any age or nation, should have been suffered to be borne away by the poorer imitators of their memorable deeds, the authors of the imperfect settlement of 1688" (*Statesmen,* xxviii).

Forster perceived two impediments to a general appreciation of the Whig view of the Commonwealth period: ignorance of English history and the misconception resulting from the bias and misstatements of early chroniclers of the events of that period, some of whom played a prominent part and, therefore, wrote self-serving accounts later. He attempted to rectify the first problem in his historical surveys—"A Treatise on the Popular Progress in English History," "A History for Young England," and "The Plantagenets and the Tudors"—focusing in each reign upon the extent to which the sovereign, weak or powerful, was forced by events to yield privileges to the people in order to consolidate his authority—perhaps over foreign interests, perhaps among powerful landowners at home. The second problem was the more severe; to correct the bias of the early chroniclers, Forster dug into long-buried or ignored official documents, diaries, and letters to explore the critical issues of the day and the personalities and motives of the primary actors: "The Civil Wars and Oliver Cromwell," "The Debates on the Grand Remonstrance," and *Arrest of the Five Members by Charles the First.*

In the opening pages of his "Debates on the Grand Remonstrance," Forster demonstrated how ignorance and self-serving authorship had combined to frustrate the truth about the founding of the Commonwealth. A typical example of early bias was Lord Clarendon's *History of the Rebellion,* which Forster said contained much "flagrant and deliberate falsification of the truth" regarding the debates in the House of Commons over the Grand Remonstrance (*Essays,* 1:108).

The dependence on such "authorities" by subsequent historians infuriated Forster, and since they proposed no "better or more intimate knowledge of the Great Remonstrance than was derivable from the garbled page of Clarendon," he set out in earnest to put matters right (*Essays,* 1:3).

Forster's techniques in writing his own biographical studies naturally varied with the scope of each project. In the surveys, for example, he provided little quoted material and no footnotes, thereby making the reader's acceptance of his views dependent wholly upon the success of his own rhetorical and ethical appeals. In the "Treatise on the Popular Progress in English History," Forster traced in twenty-one double-columned pages the history of the British monarchy from 1066 to the accession of James I in 1603. He covered almost as much ground, from 1154 through the end of James's reign in 1625, in the sixty pages of his essay "The Plantagenets and the Tudors." "A History for Young England" is the fullest of the surveys, attempting to cover one reign in each of its fourteen chapters, from 1066 to 1258. Obviously, his fundamental problem was to achieve clarity and compression simultaneously, a formidable task.

Examining these essays, a modern reader is struck by the aptness of Bulwer's comment on the longer works, that Forster has "a remarkable power of generalization, and he groups his details so as to render clear and prominent the facts he desires to enforce." The principal technique Forster used to impose form and clear direction on so immense a mass of material was, after each major example, to restate his thesis, and often to extend it slightly, in prose itself memorable and compelling.

Consider the following two extracts from "A Treatise on the Popular Progress in English History." The first argues that a principle once conceded in a specific case is forever binding also in the general cases it may later be found to cover. The specific instance here is the barons' attempt to consolidate power for themselves at the expense of King John through the provisions of the Magna Charta:

Little did they suspect that, under words that were intended to limit the relations of feudal power, many of the grandest equitable truths of polity lay concealed. . . . They denied protection to serfs, and knew not that

the swords which gave them that very power of denial had already cut
through forever the bonds of English serfdom. They protested against the
power of taxation in a prince, while they reserved it in limitation for
themselves, ignorant that the formidable principle would bear down the
weak exception. . . . A truth has not its fair side and its foul. A principle
is not a convertible thing; nor could these iron barons of Merton, all-
powerful as they were, claim its operation in the one case, and control it
in the other. All was not done when their part was done. (*Statesmen,* viii)

The second example, which follows discussion of concessions by
Henry IV two hundred years later, restates the idea of the first
passage and extends it, asserting that a principle is not lost, once
conceded, even if it is ignored or denied for a period as in the reign
of the despotic Henry VIII. This latter idea is crucial to Forster's
thesis about the unimpeded development of the rights of the people
vis-à-vis the monarchy, and he repeats the idea frequently; to him
it justified the rebellion of the Commons against Charles I:

It is vain to say that many of these vast advantages were, in later years,
obscured or disregarded. To show that they were once achieved, and that
the principle involved in them was solemnly recognised and acted on, is
to demonstrate all. . . . The struggle between two such principles as
tyranny and freedom, once set on foot, admits no compromise. A generation of men who have insisted upon certain rights for themselves,
cannot, by subsequent indolence or indifference, be said to have bargained
away those rights from a succeeding generation; nor, when the theft of a
people's liberties has been confessed by one restoration of them to the just
possessors, can any prince, into whose violent keeping they may again
have fallen, claim exemption from the penalties of political crime. The
thief and the receiver are classed together by our laws. (*Statesmen,* xi–xii)

Also clear in these two extracts is the essentially optimistic strain
in Forster's progressive view of history. This attitude is no less
apparent when he dealt with the inhumane and horrible in men's
thoughts and deeds. In "A History for Young England," for example, after extensively detailing an enormous massacre of men,
women, children, and farm animals directed by William the Con-
queror, he halted the flow of his narrative to offer the following
observation about William:

I pause to take a breath from these oppressive horrors. Strange that the
man who had so many of the gifts by which the Creator marks a leader

of men;—sagacity, penetration, immovable resolve, and not seldom a manly generosity, and temper of unswerving justice;—should thus have braved the infamy which history has rightly fastened on his name. Yet such is the mingled evil and good through which the ways of Providence vindicate themselves in the world, that it may be doubted, in that season of elemental revolution and change, if, without the infamy, we could have had the good, the glory, and the honour. There are times, in the moral as in the physical world, when the earthquake and the pestilence *must* come. . . . (368)

Nor does the optimism of positing that good must and will come out of evil keep Forster from comprehending evil and describing it in graphic detail. After pointing out the important contribution of Henry VIII in checking the Catholic Church and the influence of Rome in England, Forster concluded that the "broad and vicious body of Henry the Eighth was as the bridge between the old and new religions" (*Statesmen,* xix). But his total abhorrence of Henry's viciousness was the major tone in Forster's description of his reign, ending with the following brief, judgmental look at his last days:

It is fearful but not unsalutary to cast a parting glance at it [Henry's body] after its great work upon the earth was done. It lay immoveable and helpless, a mere corrupt and bloated mass of dying tyranny. No friend was near to comfort it; not even a courtier dared to warn it of its coming hour. The men who it had gorged with the offal of its plunder hung back in affright from its perishing agonies, in disgust from its ulcerous sores. It could not move a limb nor lift a hand. The palace doors were made wider for its passage through them; and it could only then pass by means of machinery. Yet to the last it kept its ghastly state, descended daily from bedchamber into room of kingly audience through a hole in the palace ceiling, and was nightly, by the same means, lifted back again to its sleepless bed. (*Statesmen,* xix–xx)

To Forster the progressive element in the history of the English monarchy consisted in the gradual vesting of ever more authority in Parliament, specifically in the House of Commons, culminating in the 1640s in the Long Parliament, which rose up against the tyrannical Charles I and established constitutional guarantees in a Commonwealth. Exploration of these turbulent days is the subject of Forster's detailed accounts in "The Debates on the Grand Remonstrance" and *Arrest of the Five Members by Charles the First* and, with less presentation of dramatic action, in "The Civil Wars and

Oliver Cromwell." In these more substantial studies, compression was unnecessary; indeed, in each we find lengthy quotations and footnotes, which themselves often run more than a page. Authorities on both sides of the issues are cited as well as comparatively disinterested eyewitness observers. Forster's young protégé Percy Fitzgerald described these later studies and their accompanying apparatus as "ponderous historical treatises . . . dreary things, pedantic, solemn, and heavy."[15] Bulwer's evaluation was more sympathetic and more accurate, despite his own need to demur over Forster's conclusions: "The characteristics of Mr. Forster's mind are, in many respects, eminently fitted to the subjects he selects for historical disquisition. He finds his heroes in men who were thoroughly in earnest, and earnestness is the distinguishing attribute of his own vigorous understanding. . . . His style itself is in accordance with his theme—solid and impressive; animated where occasion permits, with a severe and manly eloquence."[16]

Published with "The Debates on the Grand Remonstrance" and "The Civil Wars and Oliver Cromwell" was the survey "The Plantagenets and the Tudors." As an extension of the latter, Forster added an eleven-page sketch of James I, including some remarks about James's son, who was to become Charles I. This sketch provides necessary context for the matter of the longer works detailing events leading to the Revolution.

Forster found both monarchs odious, possessed of the worst characteristics of the preceding Tudors (Henry VII, Henry VIII, Edward IV, Mary, and Elizabeth I), but with none of their mitigating accomplishments. In the addendum to his essay, we see, reflected in the compressed style necessitated by the surveys, examples of Forster-as-advocate on the attack.

Of James I:

"Do I mak the judges? Do I mak the bishops?" he exclaimed, as the powers of his new dominion dawned on his delighted sense: "Then, God's wauns! I mak what likes me, law and gospel!" It was even so. And this license to make gospel and law was given, with other far more questionable powers, to a man whose personal appearance and qualities were as suggestive of contempt, as his public acts were provocative of rebellion. (*Essays,* 1:227)

By way of conclusion, after detailing various political, religious, and social "crimes," he added:

In the presence of such acts and utterances, it is barely an act of justice to the memory of their perpetrator to say that the sins of this complexion were only half expiated by the blood of his unhappy son. The records of civilised life offer no other instance of such pretensions amid a society of rational men. We have to turn for a parallel to the pestilential swamps of Africa, where one of those prodigious princes whom we bribe with rum and trinkets to assist us in suppressing the slave trade, announced not long ago. . . , "God made me after His image: I am all the same as God: and He appointed me a King." This was James I's creed precisely; and after delivering it to his subjects in words exactly similar, he might be publicly seen of them . . . "wallowing in beastly delights." (*Essays*, 1:238–39)

And of Charles I, James's son:

There is a complexional weakness imparted at birth, which nothing afterwards will cure; and this, disqualifying alike for stern resistance or manly submission, was unhappily a part of Charles I's most sad inheritance. He was nearly six years old before he could stand or speak, his limbs being weak and distorted, and his mouth mal-formed; nor did he ever walk quite without difficulty, or speak without a stammer. Who shall say how far these physical defects carried also with them the moral weaknesses, the vacillation of purpose and obstinacy of irresolution, and insincerity and bad faith, which so largely helped to bring him to the scaffold? (*Essays*, 1:230–31)

Here then, for Forster, was a context for rebellion. After a hundred years of Tudor reign, in which virtue and vice existed on a grand scale and England as a nation grew substantially in prestige and strength, the country had faced in James and Charles a half-century of gross abrogation of the people's rights as vested in Parliament and had suffered significant loss of strength and prestige both at home and abroad.

The bitterness that Forster felt over the reigns of James and Charles focused upon the abuse of the people's civil and religious freedoms. Hence, supremely important for him were the Grand Remonstrance and Charles's reaction, the attempt to arrest the five members of the House of Commons he believed most responsible for the document. The Grand Remonstrance was drawn up by the House as an appeal to the people to defend the concessions the powerful Parliament had won from the king when, after ruling without a

Parliament for twelve years, Charles had been forced to call it to sit to replenish his drained coffers.

The Remonstrance itself consisted of 206 Clauses itemizing the misdeeds of the king over the preceding fifteen years. Blamed for much of the mischief of those years were ministers and close personal counselors of the king not entirely loyal to him, to England, or to the Protestant religion, but motivated rather by papist sympathies and connections. To Forster's mind, the king's response to the Remonstrance exposed his character in its worst light, showing that he respected neither the people nor their chosen representatives. Charles not only filed charges of treason against five leaders of the House instrumental in drawing up and getting the Grand Remonstrance passed there, but subsequently he personally entered the Commons at the head of an assembly of armed guards, pensioners, and soldiers, attempting to apprehend in person the five members—who had slipped away only a moment before.

In "The Debates on the Grand Remonstrance," Forster's purpose was fourfold: to trace the sentiment that gave rise to the document; to rewrite the history of the debates, correcting what he deemed to be the self-serving remarks of men like Clarendon and Warwick surrounding the passing, printing, and publication of the Remonstrance; to underscore the gravity of these events and the feelings they generated; and to review the results that followed the presentation of the Remonstrance to the king and its subsequent publication to the people. One of the most significant features of this essay, one that brought into focus all that Forster had to say about the Grand Remonstrance, was a forty-page abstract of that document, the first such detailed analysis ever offered by an historian.

Forster directed most of his discussion at the king's supporters in the House, whom he usually shows being bested in debate by John Pym or John Hampden, but Forster does give a brief glimpse of the king when the Remonstrance is presented, providing a summary of the king's actions at that time. Forster mentions that the king received cordially the committee that presented him the Remonstrance, although he pressed them for details of what they intended to do with the document. Immediately after receiving the committee, he sent word to Commons not to publish the Remonstrance until he had had a chance to respond—which according to Forster he never intended to do, except through the specific steps he immediately took to weaken and intimidate Parliament and to assert his power:

> He told the Committee that he did not at that time design to answer their Remonstrance, yet there was hardly an act at this moment contemplated by him . . . which did not practically express his answer. It was in his proclamation for obedience to the laws regulating worship, in his order for the dismissal of the City Guard over the houses, in his direction that they should in future be guarded by the bands of Westminster and Middlesex officered by his own servants, and in his proposed removal of Balfour from the command of the Tower. . . . Many to whom even the voting of the Remonstrance had appeared of doubtful expediency, now saw and admitted the necessity of publishing it to the people. (*Essays,* 1:145)

Accordingly, within another month the Grand Remonstrance was published, and on January 4, 1642, came the king's fateful response, when he attempted, as Forster said, to seize "with his own hand upon five members of the House of Commons sitting in their places in Parliament, against whom, on the day preceding, he had exhibited in the Upper House, through his Attorney General, articles of impeachment for high treason" (*Arrest,* 1).

The *Arrest of the Five Members by Charles the First* deals with this effort to charge high treason on the five members of the House of Commons most active in the Remonstrance and with its surrounding debates. The work is Forster's longest history, 486 pages printed as if it were published in the seventeenth century with typeface and format characteristic of the period ("f" and "s" printed as virtually the same letter), marginal notes, and lengthy footnotes. It is full of scenes of violence and actions prompted by the fear of violence, especially in its recording of mob scenes outside the House of Commons and in the City's streets. Throughout, the inevitability of armed conflict produces a palpable tension; perhaps no scenes more powerfully show this tension than those descriptions of the king arriving with an armed band numbering better than 200 to enter the House and forcibly arrest Pym, Hampden, Strode, Hasselrig, and Hollis. Forster's description is panoramic: the door of the House is thrown open and the king walks to the Speaker's chair as all rise and doff their hats in strained deference; the king speaks and the deference disappears; as he departs, so does all decorum, and cries of "Privilege! Privilege!" fill the air around him.

Forster describes at some length the subsequent efforts of the king to arrest the five and dwells upon the fact that their popularity among their colleagues and with the masses grew such that the king had to waive the impeachment proceedings and later all efforts to prosecute. Forster pointedly observes that while the king even granted a pardon to the five, never did he allow them to prove in court their innocence and never did he formally withdraw the original charge of treason. These actions seemed to Forster perfect evidence of the king's tyranny, confirmation of the characteristics Forster ascribed to him in the essay on the Plantagenets and Tudors—"moral weakness, vacillation of purpose, obstinacy of resolution, insincerity and bad faith"—and perfect justification for opposition, even at the price of armed conflict and regicide.

"The Civil Wars and Oliver Cromwell" is an expanded version of the essay that appeared in the *Edinburgh Review* for January 1856. This ostensibly was a review of three books by M. Guizot—*Histoire de la Republique d'Angleterre et de Cromwell, Richard Cromwell,* and *History of Oliver Cromwell and the English Commonwealth*—and a volume by George Bankes, M.P., *The Story of Corfe Castle, collected from ancient Chronicles and Records; also from the private memoirs of a Family Resident there in the time of the Civil Wars.* Forster used the books to provide his own disquisition on their subjects.

Forster quickly dismissed the Bankes volume, for Bankes had defended the royalist position as represented by Charles's principal minister, Strafford, who had been put to death as a traitor early in the sitting of the Long Parliament. Forster charged Bankes with misunderstanding the evidence he presented and with selecting, as did Clarendon, evidence neither truthful nor objective. The principal interest of "The Civil Wars and Oliver Cromwell," however, is the Protector, himself. Forster was most respectful of the books by the French statesman Guizot, whose thesis he endorsed: "God does not grant to the great men who have set on disorder the foundations of their greatness, the power to regulate at their pleasure and for centuries, even according to their better desires, the government of nations" (*Essays,* 1:286).

The issue, of course, was Cromwell—how to understand his character. Forster briefly reviewed several judgments, the one held by most earlier historians, the one he himself formerly subscribed to during the 1830s,[17] the one growing out of Carlyle's study of Cromwell's speeches and letters in 1845, which radically altered

Forster's own views, and finally that of Guizot. In the abstract prose of generalized portrait Forster presented the following description of Carlyle's vision of the hero-patriot, an assessment of Cromwell that Forster had come to share with that other famous historian and biographer:

. . . Cromwell was no hypocrite or actor of plays, had no vanity or pride in the prodigious intellect he possessed, was no theorist in politics or government, was no victim of ambition, was no seeker after sovereignty or temporal power. That he was a man whose every thought was with the Eternal,—a man of great, robust, massive mind, and of an honest, stout, English heart; subject to melancholy for the most part, because of the deep yearnings of his soul for the sense of divine forgiveness, but inflexible and resolute always, because in all things governed by the supreme law. That in him was seen a man whom no fear but of the divine anger could distract; whom no honour in man's bestowal could seduce or betray; who knew the duty of the hour to be ever imperative, and who sought only to do the work, whatever it might be, whereunto he believed God to have called him. (*Essays,* 1:283)

Were his writing limited to such characteristic examples of nine-teenth-century historical style, Forster's histories would offer a modern reader little satisfaction; fortunately, he always added to his abstractions some human touch to bring the biographical portraits to life. It is one thing to read the encomiums; it is another to see visibly before us Speaker Lenthal, for example, in the House of Commons, stalwart in his resistance to the might of an angry monarch standing an arm's length away. When asked by the king if the five men he is seeking are present in the hall and later if the speaker knows where they may be found, Lenthal, kneeling in deference to his king, says: "I have neither eyes to see nor tongue to speak in this place, but as the House directs me, whose servant I am here; and I humbly beg your majesty's pardon that I cannot give any other answer than this to what your majesty is pleased to demand of me" (*Arrest,* 191–92).

Such a touch redeems the superlative praise of the Protector, even as Forster removed the last blot on the Protector's escutcheon by denying that Cromwell was unfaithful to his wife–a vicious royalist lie, Forster declared, that even Guizot was tricked into believing. In Cromwell's defense, Forster quoted the single extant letter from

Cromwell's wife to her husband, reputedly the words of a woman who knew that her jealousy was justified:

My dearest . . . I wonder you should blame me for writing no oftener, when I have sent three for one: I cannot but think they are miscarried. Truly, if I know my own heart, I should as soon neglect myself as to omit the least thought towards you, when in doing it I must do it to myself. But when I do write, my dear, I seldom have any satisfactory answer, which makes me think my writing is slighted; as well it may; but I cannot but think your love covers my weakness and infirmities. Truly my life is but half a life in your absence. (*Essays,* 1:332)

Forster's conclusion was typically unequivocal: "That is not the writing of a woman jealous of anything but the share of her husband's time and care which public affairs steal from her" (332).

Historical Biographer

Forster's historical biographies, except for the 1864 volumes on Sir John Eliot, appeared in two series in the 1830s. These constitute his earliest historical work and examine the lives of seven men: John Pym, Sir John Eliot, Sir Henry Vane, Thomas Wentworth (the Earl of Strafford), John Hampden, Henry Marten, and Oliver Cromwell. All served in Parliament during the reign of Charles I; all except Eliot, who died in the Tower in 1632 after having been imprisoned by Charles, participated in the momentous actions of the Long Parliament (1640–1653); all began as patriots in the popular cause and, excepting Strafford and Cromwell (as Forster conceived his character at this time), remained so throughout their careers; all interested Forster because either they supported personal freedoms guaranteed by law and vested principally in Parliament or they opposed these freedoms in the interest of a tyrannical monarchy or a military dictatorship; all, patriots and despots alike, were intelligent, educated, courageous, powerful, and extraordinarily charismatic individuals.

A brief survey of the two series, "Our Early Patriots" in *Englishman's Magazine* and *Lives of Eminent British Statesmen* in Lardner's *Cabinet Cyclopaedia,* reveals the same point of view that Forster developed in his more extensive histories: the faithful patriots among these seven statesmen were the most courageous and glorious individuals ever to sit in a position of authority in the English kingdom; this period of history was more important than any other because of the inordinate sacrifices these great men made to secure fundamental civil and religious liberties for all Englishmen.

An essentially didactic purpose—using the past to teach the present—governed all of Forster's historical writing. For the narrowing of his focus to the personal lives of great men, he offered a slightly more specific rationale and added a disclaimer: too much of the recorded history of the Commonwealth period either had been colored by partisan views or confined primarily to discussion of legal and constitutional issues. Too little time had been given to the "private motives" and "personal histories" of the great men of the age. Influenced by Carlyle's view of history as biography, Forster set out in the briefer sketches, and, too, in the longer biographies, to offer "portraiture of such individual character,—which will be found to illustrate forcibly those principles of right conduct, that have contributed, in all ages, to the best purposes of usefulness"; in doing so, he disclaimed "all quarrel with truth," and affirmed that he would "in every case prefer its discovery to the assertion of a favourite opinion" ("Our Early Patriots," 351).

Despite this disclaimer, Forster was as much an advocate in the early sketches as he would later be in the histories. These patriots were honest, courageous men of unquestioned integrity who "for the destruction of the corruption of *that* day, risked their all, and on the justice and benefit of its abolition pledged their fame to the latest posterity" ("Our Early Patriots," 351). John Pym, who brought about Strafford's execution for treason and who later led the debates on the Grand Remonstrance, was to Forster an "eloquent" orator, a "great statesman," and "patriot," the "most popular" man of his time ("John Pym," 510, 511); even "Charles himself ever delighted to refer to the unpublished speeches of Pym as to a text book of constitutional principles" (511). Forster energetically celebrated Sir John Eliot, the "first great martyr to the cause of freedom,"[18] who brought proceedings against the Duke of Buckingham, Charles's especial favorite, and later opposed the king on both religious and taxation issues; Forster called his exertions "glorious"; he was himself "illustrious and high-minded," and in his life "none was more honest, more brave, more generously attached to his country," than he ("Sir John Eliot," 623, 635, 636). The "manly," "enthusiastic," "eloquent," and "immortal" Henry Vane devised a system for parliamentary reform only to have it appropriated by the "hypocritical tyrant and military usurper," Cromwell, who muttered aloud when driving Vane from the House: "Sir Harry Vane! Sir Harry Vane! the Lord deliver me from Sir Harry Vane!" ("Sir Henry Vane," 1, 2, 11, 13).

Such inflated praise of Pym, Eliot, and Vane and also of Henry Marten and John Hampden was qualified little in the fuller portraits Forster drew of them in his *Lives of Eminent British Statesmen* for Lardner's *Cabinet Cyclopaedia* (1836–1839). The portraits given in these later volumes seem more palatable, however, because they are leavened by the lives of Strafford and Cromwell, men, who though powerfully attractive, were in Forster's view essentially villains, and because Forster gathered a welter of details for the longer studies. Each of the five volumes for Lardner ran 400 to 420 pages. The first three contained two biographies apiece; the last two were devoted to Cromwell.

The factual material in the texts was amply underpinned by frequent lengthy and scholarly footnotes and by numerous appendixes, which included speeches, legal documents, and even a transcript of the topics of Strafford's final remarks delivered to the crowd from the scaffold where he was beheaded. Letters and personal diaries, too, are an important source of factual information and of character analysis in the *Cyclopaedia* volumes. Such material abounds in the text and footnotes and represents a crucial element in Forster's theory of biography. He often argued the value of such documents in reviews of others' works, and we will see later in his literary biographies, also, the extensive use he made of such autobiographical material.

The relationship between the earlier 1831 sketches of Pym, Eliot, and Vane and the later full portraits in the *Cyclopaedia* consists primarily of the repetition of some incidents, with substantial expansion in the later volumes, and in many instances of language borrowed from the earlier descriptions. The material on Sir John Eliot constitutes an instance of such repetition and expansion, one that illustrates an important characteristic of Forster's biographies: his ability to shape material so that even faults may become virtues in a man whose overall life proved worthy in Forster's estimation. Eliot is described as a young man of "strong passions and ardent temper." His early keen friendship with the obnoxious duke of Buckingham was not a serious obstacle for his biographer because Eliot later did all he could to wrest power and influence from that rogue favorite of Charles. More of a problem was the rash act of the young Eliot in stabbing a neighbor in that gentleman's house in retaliation for some tales the man had told on the youth to his father. In the version in *Englishman's Magazine,* Forster offered the following rather unsatisfactory description and explanation: ". . . it will appear that Mr. Moyle used certain taunting expressions, too haughty to be borne by the proud spirit of Eliot, who, in a moment of rash and wayward passion, drew his rapier and made a pass at the old enemy of his house. Fortunately the thrust did not take fatal effect; and, with the characteristic impulse of a generous mind, Eliot hastened to make atonement" ("Sir John Eliot," 624). The atonement is a written apology: ". . . it is addressed to Mr. Moyle and is subscribed by some of the most eminent men in Cornwall. Its humble terms do honour to the writer; he confesses that it was a hasty but unpremeditated act of violence, and speaks the better feelings of a noble mind chastised from its ungoverned passions" (624). This weak effort to mitigate a genuinely serious and repulsive act was substantially buttressed—although along entirely similar lines—in the expanded treatment accorded it in the later version for the *Cyclopaedia.*

Another instance showing Forster manipulating material to the benefit of his favorites involves an early discussion of John Pym in *Englishman's Magazine* that turned out to be entirely erroneous; the strongly favorable conclusion Forster drew there about the character of Pym and others was threatened. Writing in 1831, Forster had emphatically insisted that Pym, Cromwell, and Hampden, along with others, having become convinced that life in England was intolerable and that Charles would continue to rule indefinitely without a Parliament, decided in 1638 to flee England for the New World:

Certain it is that Pym . . . Hampden, Oliver Cromwell, and others, had absolutely embarked with many followers on board eight vessels bound for New England . . . ; the vessels were under weigh when an order from the council board arrested their departure! The hand of fate was upon Charles; the disappointed patriots leaped again upon their native shore, inspired with fiercer resolution, and binding themselves to each other by an ominous pledge, that, "though in the contest, monarchy and the monarch should fall together, it was their duty to persevere," and wait for the contingency that must inevitably summon a Parliament. ("John Pym," 502)

While writing Pym's life for the *Cyclopaedia,* Forster discovered that the incident had never occurred. Nevertheless, he used this "rumour of history" to make as strong a case for his heroes as he had done originally, and his language is equally authoritarian:

Were this anecdote authentic, the hand of fate had been visible upon Charles indeed! But there is no good authority for it, and it is deficient in all the moral evidences of truth. The mind cannot bring itself to imagine the spirits of such men as these yielding so easily to the despair of the country; and at this moment Hampden was the "argument of all tongues" for his resistance to ship-money, while to Pym the vision of the fatal meeting to which he had summoned Wentworth now became daily more and more distinct. (*Cyclopaedia,* 3:81)

Examples such as these show the weaknesses in Forster's advocacy. More important are the strengths of Forster's *Lives,* which define his best accomplishments. He was often a man of extraordinary sensitivity who could perceive the complexities surrounding human motivations and actions—especially in the lives of great men. His studies of Strafford and Cromwell show this understanding best; in them he captured quite remarkably that blending of good and evil that both attracts and repels, often rendering the necessary passing of moral judgment very difficult. Forster could see the human dignity of a person we would expect such a dogmatic chronicler to despise. His treatment of the execution of Charles, the tyrant king, provides a typical instance:

Through the whole of that scene Charles bore himself with a dignified composure, and was to the last undisturbed, self-possessed, and serene. He addressed the crowd from the scaffold, forgave all his enemies, protested that the war was not begun by him, declared that the people's right was only to have their life and goods their own, "a share in the government being nothing pertaining to them," and concluded with words which, perhaps, expressed a sincere delusion, that "he died the martyr of the people." When his head fell, severed by the executioner at one blow, "a dismal, universal groan issued from the crowd." (*Cyclopaedia,* 4:314)

This powerful scene develops virtually without condemnation of Charles. Forster retained the same tone in his subsequent comments, where he conceded that this death was "a most melancholy and disastrous error," but one committed in "good faith" as a "terrible example," and not without cause. Slowly, but inexorably, Forster runs through the litany of Charles's crimes; the catalog speaks for itself, matter-of-factly, allowing the tone of sadness, not of hatred or contempt, to remain. The conclusion is unavoidable: Charles conspired against the liberty of the country in an "intense desire for absolute power and authority" (*Cyclopaedia*, 4:315).

The ability to cause the reader to feel a common humanity between himself and one ultimately to be judged a despot is most evident in the studies of Strafford and Cromwell, both of whom Forster condemned.

Forster presented Thomas Wentworth, the earl of Strafford, as an inordinately accomplished statesman who had once, before his apostasy to the popular cause, been a great friend of Pym's and had opposed certain of the king's actions, at one point suffering imprisonment for refusing the monarch a loan. Having shown Strafford to be made of noble stuff, Forster then presented his moving to the royalist position, and using his powerful charm, imagination, ambitious spirit, and bold resolve to attain much in Charles's behalf, rising accordingly to exalted rank, and, by the time he was accused of high treason by Pym, holding the positions of Lord President of the Council for York, Lord Lieutenant of Ireland, and Chief Minister to the king in England. Forster presented him as a man who had assumed virtually absolute power in the service of an absolute monarch. Using this authority in Ireland, for example, he restructured the country's commerce and industry, strengthened the number and discipline of the army, and secured to the crown much additional land and estates. While acknowledging Strafford's accomplishments, Forster stressed that to attain these ends, Strafford had seriously abrogated the rights of the people of Ireland, dealing with that country as if it were merely a conquered land, and, in effect, had rendered himself an outlaw in the eyes of powerful men in the House of Commons.

In 1640, when the king was finally reduced to calling a Parliament, Pym knew that the first blow must be struck at the king's powerful minister—Strafford. It is in the description of the fifteen-day trial of Strafford as conducted by Pym that Forster created some of his most moving and dramatic moments, allowing the reader to understand fully the enormous importance of the events, the strengths and weaknesses of these grand antagonists, and the dignity and integrity of great minds absolutely committed to opposite positions.

In this contest, Strafford was defeated, despite Charles's written guarantee of safety and the king's efforts to intrude personally in his behalf. Nevertheless, through the repeated eloquence of Strafford's statements—in his own defense, in letters to his family, on the scaffold at his execution—and in descriptions of certain technical aspects of the trial itself, Forster assured that the reader's sympathy would, to some extent, always be elicited for Strafford, despite the fact that Forster himself agreed wholly with Pym that Stafford's life was justly forfeited.

Moreover, Forster lets the reader see that the case was stacked against Stafford, even if the basic cause was valid. Some of the twenty-eight charges involved recollections of what Strafford had said in informal conversations as well as in formal council meetings and in other conversations; others concerned decisions he had taken part in only as one member of a judicial court. The object of the trial was to demonstrate "an attempt to subvert the fundamental laws" of the country:

Their course—to deduce a legal construction of treason from actions notoriously gone 'through' with in the service and in exaltation of the king— was to show that, no matter with what motive, any actions undertaken which had a tendency to prove destructive to the state, amounted, in legal effect, to a traitorous design against the sovereign. The sovereign, it was argued by these great men, could never have had a contemplated existence beyond, or independent of, the state. (*Cyclopaedia,* 2:383–84)

Forster showed the reader that, beyond this general strategy for defining treason, Pym had further disabled Strafford's case by having the bishops withdraw from the trial, by debarring Strafford's major witness in his defense from the proceedings by charging him with treason, by having Strafford's counsel restricted to the argument only of points of law, and by removing the oath of secrecy protecting the king's council. Hence, Forster demonstrated that the outcome of the trial was largely a foregone conclusion.

Even so, Strafford, physically disabled by crippling disease, was eloquent in his own defense, and Forster preserved some of his remarks, both at the trial and in other contexts. In effect, though Forster himself would not defend Strafford's life with his own words, he was willing to let Strafford speak in his own behalf. Referring to the use of words spoken in the secrecy accorded members of the king's council, Strafford is heard to declare:

My lords, these words were not wantonly or unnecessarily spoken, or whispered in a corner, but they were spoken in full council, where, by the duty of my oath, I was obliged to speak, according to my heart and conscience, in all things concerning the king's service. If I had foreborne to speak what I conceived to be for the benefit of the king and the people, I had been perjured towards Almighty God; and for delivering my mind openly and freely, shall I be in danger of my life as a traitor? If that necessity be put upon me, I thank God, by his blessing, I have learned not to stand in fear of him who can only kill the body. If the question be, whether I must be traitor to man, or perjured to God, I will be faithful to my creator; and whatsoever shall befall me from popular rage or from my own weakness, I must leave it to that almighty being, and to the justice and honour of my judges. (*Cyclopaedia,* 2:390)

Equally powerful and affecting are words Forster quoted from a letter Strafford wrote to his eldest son, whom he advised "to be not discouraged" but

to give all respect to my wife, that hath ever had a great love unto you, and therefore will be well becoming you. Never be awanting in your love and care to your sisters, but let them ever be most dear unto you: —for this will give others cause to esteem and respect you for it, and it is a duty that you owe them in the memory of your excellent mother and myself. . . . Sweet Will, be careful to take the advice of those friends, which are by me desired to advise you for your education. (*Cyclopaedia,* 2:406–7)

In addition, Forster recited Strafford's last words to his brother at the scaffold:

"Brother . . . what do you see in me to cause these tears? Does any innocent fear betray in me—guilt? or my innocent boldness—atheism? . . . No thoughts on envy, no dreams of treason, nor jealousies, nor cares for the king, the state, or myself, shall interrupt this easy sleep. Remember me to my sister, and to my wife, and carry my blessing to my eldest son, and to Ann, and Arabella, not forgetting my little infant, that knows neither good nor evil, and cannot speak for itself. God speak for it, and bless it!" (*Cyclopaedia,* 2:409–10)

Clearly, Forster intended to be fair.

Concluding this chapter with an examination of Forster's life of Oliver Cromwell is singularly fitting. As we have seen, Forster's primary objective in each of his historical studies was to memorialize the "Statesmen of the Commonwealth," those geniuses in the popular cause who were the "great authors of all the legislative triumphs . . . and indeed of all the essential political liberty that our country has enjoyed" (*Cyclopaedia*, 7:127). The historical importance of these men, as Forster judged them, is crucial in understanding his assessment of Cromwell, for the evils of Strafford and Charles, in Forster's mind at this time, paled before those of Cromwell. At his death, not only were all his "vast designs" for the English people and their constitution "sunk with him into the grave," but ". . . he dragged there, too, in so far as it was possible for him to do so— for a *good* as well as great thought, once born in the world, can never *wholly* die,—the more virtuous and more able designs of the yet immortal statesmen he supplanted, and left the path altogether clear for the base, the wicked, and licentious slavery, of the restored monarch who succeeded him" (*Cyclopaedia*, 6:191–92). The question Forster set out to answer was, why? How could a man endowed with the range of capabilities Cromwell possessed become so utterly a tyrant?

To answer that question Forster initiated the most comprehensive inquiry into the life and mind of Cromwell attempted to that time. Forster employed letters, diaries, firsthand accounts—from Cromwell's troops, from members of Parliament, from the clergy, from friends and enemies alike; tales, legends, and myths were examined; the works of subsequent historians were cited; official documents were culled; over and over the Protector's own words were quoted and scrutinized. And Forster took pains to render the story, displaying one grand, panoramic scene after another: Cromwell before his 1,000-man, hand-picked army; scenes of battle in a terrible Civil War ending in regicide; triumphs and defeats involving glorious deeds and enormous bloodletting—all of it symbolically dissolved and made pointless, Forster insisted, on April 20, 1653, when, at a given signal, the door of the House of Commons was flung open, revealing "five or six files of musketeers with their arms ready" (*Cyclopaedia*, 7:62). From then on we see the man who refused to be king become instead even more odious and inflexibly dictatorial than the monarch he had dispatched.

As in the case of Strafford, Forster never denied the attraction of Cromwell, nor did he underestimate his accomplishments and natural abilities: "Viewed in his separate qualities, a greater man has

probably never lived—a man with more eminent abilities for statesmanship—a more masterly soldier . . . . : a person more wonderfully gifted in all the attributes of subtlest thought, and of an
intellect the most piercing and profound. . . . His eminent and
thoughtful sagacity has never been disputed, nor the vastness of his
comprehension, nor the marvelous intrepidity of his purposes, nor
the inexhaustible expedients and powers of his mind" (*Cyclopaedia*,
6:190–91).

How could an individual thus talented, and possessed in addition
of the strongest conceivable religious conviction, fail? Forster's answer: "WANT OF TRUTH" (*Cyclopaedia*, 6:191). The portrait of Cromwell presented in these volumes is that of a man who, despite all
of his admirable characteristics, had at his core a character, in Forster's words, duplicitous, deceitful, sinister, crafty, and hypocritical.
Forster built his arguments slowly, over Cromwell's entire career,
revealing a character full of moral complexity and ambiguity. In
Cromwell's favor, in Forster's view, were his religious convictions,
the utter confidence placed in him by patriots known to have been
unblemished in their own commitment to the people's rights, and
his uncanny ability to produce calm and apparent stability in the
face of imminent disaster, whether on the battlefield or in the House
of Commons, through various means, all of which seem ultimately
to derive from personal charisma.

But for Forster the negative case is finally confirmed in Cromwell's
relationship with the army and with Parliament. Forster charted
this hypocritical relationship at great length, demonstrating Cromwell's falseness through letters and other commentary from persons
who witnessed his deeds. For instance, Cromwell would protest
before each group that his absolute fealty to it placed his life in
danger from the other. Such duplicity could not last, of course:

It was discovered, and the presbyterians arranged a plot . . . to have their
deceiver moved to the Tower. But his affairs were ripe at last for action.
He left London suddenly; was received by the great body of the army with
acclamations; suppressed a really dangerous mutiny that threatened for the
instant to thwart his plans, by riding up in the face of the mutineers,
selecting twelve of the ringleaders, and shooting one on the instant; brought
up some regiments afterward within reach of Westminster, purged the
Parliament, and seized the king. (*Cyclopaedia*, 6:157)

But a simplistic depiction of a great man who, for whatever reasons, lost his way and stumbled into darkness and fury was never Forster's intention, and just as he recognized with Charles and, especially, with Strafford the dignified endings of their lives, so, too, he did not withhold what was known of Cromwell's death scene.

Forster had wondered more than once whether Cromwell might have been his own biggest dupe, whether his messianic vision might not have deluded him. Certainly the death scene as presented by Forster is not one of remorse or repentance. It may be read as revealing a man approaching the next life confident of all that he bore witness to in this; or it may be read with far greater ambiguity, leaving the reader to wonder about the soundness of the Lord Protector's sense of himself and his accomplishments:

Then, as they stood around his bed, he suddenly lifted himself up, and, with what energy remained, "Tell me," said he to Sterry, one of his chaplains, *"is it possible to fall from grace?"* *"It is not possible,"* replied the minister. *"Then,"* exclaimed the dying man, *"I am safe: for I know that I was once in grace."* So re-assuring himself even then with the most fatal doctrine of his life, he turned round and prayed, not for himself, but for God's people. "Lord," he said, "although I am a miserable and wretched creature, I am in covenant with thee, through grace, and I may, I will, come to thee for thy people. Thou hast made me (though very unworthy) a mean instrument to do them some good, and thee service. . . ." (*Cyclopaedia,* 7:389)

Regardless, Forster's thoughts were fixed on this world. Cromwell's prayer is not the point of rest in this biography. Instead, Forster concluded with a description of the storm that occurred on the night of Cromwell's death, deliberately describing it as similar to that awful and foreboding storm promising "dire combustion and confused events" that swept the land the night of Duncan's death in *Macbeth.* "It was," he said of the evening of Cromwell's passing, "a night which prophesied a woeful time to England" (*Cyclopaedia,* 7:392).

Chapter Four
Literary Biographer
Eighteenth-Century Authors

Forster's work as biographer of literary figures did not begin until the 1840s, after he had established himself as an historian of the Commonwealth period of the seventeenth century and as one of the chief literary critics of his own day. His interest in literary biography centered, however, upon figures from neither of these periods, but upon eighteenth-century authors: Charles Churchill, Daniel Defoe, Samuel Foote, Oliver Goldsmith, Richard Steele, and Jonathan Swift. The "lives" of Churchill and Defoe and of Foote and Steele first appeared as review essays in the *Edinburgh Review* and the *Quarterly,* respectively,[1] having been occasioned by books Forster believed failed to treat these men justly. His studies of Goldsmith and Swift were amply documented, volume-length biographies;[2] the latter, projected for three volumes, was cut short after the first volume by Forster's death. *The Life and Adventures of Oliver Goldsmith* (1848) received such enthusiastic response that Forster began almost immediately to expand it for a two-volume second edition entitled *The Life and Times of Oliver Goldsmith* and published in 1854. Yet, despite his research—ten years on Goldsmith and twenty on Swift—and the popularity particularly of the *Goldsmith,* Forster is best known today not for biographies of eighteenth-century writers, but for the volumes on his most famous literary contemporary—Charles Dickens. In his last years, Forster exercised what was, in effect, a moral imperative to record the lives of two literary contemporaries whom he had known for three decades—Walter Savage Landor, who died in 1864 and whose "life" Forster published in two volumes in 1869, and Dickens, who died in 1870 and whose *Life* appeared in three volumes, 1872–1874.[3]

Forster's literary biographies, therefore, fall into two categories—those of eighteenth-century writers and those of his contemporaries, Landor and Dickens. The eighteenth-century studies include sketches of Churchill, Defoe, Foote, and Steele, and a single full portrait, that of Goldsmith. The sketches provide an excellent opportunity for describing Forster's theory of biography. Not surprisingly, we can see in these studies attitudes and techniques that we have found elsewhere in his works.

The lives he records were of men whose writings he admired because their subjects and attitudes seemed to him to be "right." He painted idealized portraits, having found, through a sensitive reading of each author's best work, that his essential character was moral and optimistic, as Forster's aesthetics required. Like Carlyle, Ruskin, and Browning, Forster believed that great literature portrayed a moral world and did so because its author was at heart moral. The man might have weaknesses in his character, but they were important only insofar as they revealed what he had had to overcome. For Forster, the primary function of biographical detail was to reveal this essential moral bent. He did not believe that the biographer should report all of the evil a man might have done or that he should attempt to balance evenly the good with the bad, but rather that he should discover what best indicated the man's true nature as revealed in his works, and seeing that, insure that it would receive its due emphasis: ". . . if the strict rule were applied universally, never to accept unreservedly what is good in a man, and praise it accordingly, without minute measuring-off of what may also be condemned for evil, with detraction at least equal to the praise, there would be altogether an end at last to all just judgments, and a woful general confusion of right and wrong" ("Steele," 113).

In a sense, then, Forster the advocate is guilty of arranging the biographical facts of his authors (as distinct from his critical judgment of individual works) in a selective manner, involving suppression and even distortion. As James A. Davies has remarked on this point,

Goldsmith's envy, coarseness in company, extravagant gambling, and failure to honor contracts; Churchill's hatred and harrying of Smollett and vindictive satirical attacks on the man who thwarted him of his father's living, his participation in the rites at Medmenham Abbey, the hedonism of his epitaph; Defoe's uncontrollable anger; Foote, fat and flabby, leaving his estate to his illegitimate sons; Steele's heavy drinking, homicidal dueling, monetary marriage, illegitimate children, and flagrant dishonesty; Swift as absentee parish priest, and congenital misanthrope—all are silently omitted from Forster's pages.[4]

And it is true, as Davies notes, that Forster would slant his studies in order to make his authors more acceptable to middle-class Victorians who might be unable otherwise accurately to gauge the man's true spirit in his works. To Forster, one could convey the essential truth, but one would have to know how one's readers would respond to individual details, and so know what to include and exclude, if one were to succeed. Forster's idealized portraits are meant to do just that. He would not have considered himself misleading the public with his methods; rather, he would have argued, he was leading them more truthfully than otherwise might be the case. Like the artist in Pater's essay on "Style," Forster thought it not enough to ask if something were a fact, but whether that fact, that action, that word, would do the true thing to the reader, convey the true idea. Forster had his own unified vision of the man to convey—a vision he found corroborated in the author's best literary work—and, Victorian artist that Forster was, he would use only those details that would convey his vision into the reader's mind.

On the other hand, he does not altogether fail to note character weaknesses in his authors or flaws in their works. His studies are not "lives of saints." For example, in the biographical sketches we find that Churchill abandoned his clerical responsibilities after being ordained and, in addition, left home and wife, eventually living until his death with another woman; in his writing, he too often engaged in personal invective. Defoe did not always penetrate to the heart of a moral question; the "practical and earnest features of his character" denied him access to "that highest reach and grace of intellect" ("De Foe," 31); in his writings, he was generally unsuccessful in verse, moral essays, and theatrical criticism. Foote was mastered by the "habit of jesting and contempt, and of looking always at the ludicrous and sarcastic side," a weakness that proved "hurtful and degrading to his own nature" ("Foote," 304). And we glimpse Steele, through the eyes of Swift and Macaulay (whose book praises Addison at Steele's expense), dicing himself into a sponging-house, drinking himself into a fever, and confounding himself with debts. Yet we may consider the tableau Forster presented at the end of his study of Churchill as an apt statement of the value of such negative biographical details when juxtaposed with the spirit of the writer expressed in his work. We find Byron looking at the grave of Churchill some fifty years after the earlier poet's death, ruminating on "the Glory and the Nothing of a Name": "But a name is *not* an illusion, when it has been won by any strenuous exertion either of thought or action in an honest purpose. Time's purgatorial fire may weaken the strength of the characters it is written in, but it eats out of them also their mistakes and vices; and BYRON might have had greater hope for the living, and less pity for the dead, at the grave of CHARLES CHURCHILL" ("Churchill," 291). These lines offer a succinct synthesis of major elements in Forster's theory of literary biography: honest striving results in the successful creation of positive and moral literature and confirms an author's right to a substantial literary reputation, if not always immortality; through time, the character of the man as defined in his best and most enduring works will predominate over any personal weaknesses, which, never crucially important, may be expected to fade quickly to indistinction.

Forster's portraits were idealized, then, in that he emphasized in these biographies those positive attributes of the writers that he believed to be embodied in their works. Further, his interest in these men centers almost exclusively upon them as men-of-letters, and we seldom find biographical detail unrelated to their professional lives. The personal characteristics delineated and the methods used to present these lives closely resemble those in the historical biographies. Ultimately each man stands before us courageous, independent, and uncompromised. To mark yet another parallel, Forster, in the same manner in which he viewed British history as moving toward an ever-increasing vesting of the rights of the populace in an all-powerful House of Commons, viewed literary history from the time of Dryden as moving from dependence upon patronage and the whim of capricious and greedy publishers and booksellers to the control of a middle-class readership increasingly able to appreciate literary and social value and to dictate through their purchases the authors to be rewarded. Forster's emphasis, of course, touched both the dignity of literature as a profession and the importance of middle-class values. Each of the eighteenth-century writers he discussed acted as Dryden had by committing himself solely to the profession of literature for his livelihood: "Dryden was the first writer of any significance who composedly faced the world on the solid and settled basis of literary pursuits. . . . Literature was his trade: he not only lived upon its wages, but was never ashamed to own it. . . . It was a man's own fault after this, if he was thought disreputable because he wrote for bread. I hope that all who live by literature, are on this point grateful and unforgetful."[5]

Unfortunately, the transition from powerful patron to powerful reading public was a slow one, and the writers on whom Forster concentrated fell into the "sorry and helpless interval (so filled with calamities of authors) when the patron was completely gone, and the public had not fairly come" ("Churchill," 225). It was upon the struggle for dignity, respectability, and financial reward that Forster directed most of his attention.

Of the biographical sketches, those of Charles Churchill (1731–1764) and Samuel Foote (1720–1777) are less remarkable than those of Daniel Defoe (1661–1731) and Richard Steele (1675–1729).[6] The works of the former were little read in Forster's time; Foote had become virtually unknown. Yet even a brief examination of Forster's narrative of the life of Churchill, though the record of but a minor figure, shows a way of viewing these literary heroes that became the typical pattern throughout the biographies. At first glance, Charles Churchill offered Forster a personal life ill suited to serve as an heroic model for a middle-class readership. Forster's success with this study depended almost entirely upon his ability to persuade the reader to accept his conviction that moral literature can be written only by one whose "heart was in the right place" ("Churchill," 269).

Early in his schooling, Churchill showed a marked interest and skill in both scholarship and versification, but, as Forster was quick to establish, an impetuous marriage to a temperamentally unsuitable wife, compounded by his yielding to his father's wishes that he become a clergyman, in effect deafened him to the call of literature. What we have in Churchill is a man of the right given nature whom circumstances were leading astray. When in due time Churchill turned his back on both wife (and the creditors she and he had accumulated) and his religious vocation (he was undistinguished and unhappy as a prelate), many, then and later, viewed these acts as additional instances of rash and inexcusable abdication of responsibility. But, as Forster insisted, clearly Churchill had become enmeshed in these responsibilities through poor judgment in his youth; hence, it was at least no disgrace to leave the pulpit upon his father's death.

Lured to town life and to literature by a friend, himself attempting a literary career, and by memories of earlier accomplishments in writing, Churchill soon established a formal break with his wife and received, almost simultaneously, rejections of his first two literary efforts by the book publishers. He persevered, and of his third literary effort, *The Rosciad,* he was so confident that in the face of consistent rejections he determined to finance its publication himself. This satire on the actors and the theater of his day was an instant success.

Financial success enabled him to pay all his debts and to settle agreeably with, but apart from, his wife. Excesses occasionally followed in his lifestyle (he lived the rest of his life with a woman whose family would not take her back after he had seduced her) and his writing (through personal invective, for example, in his attack on Hogarth in the *Epistle to Hogarth*). But in *The Rosciad* and in his satires on the Scots (*The Prophecy of Famine*) and on the Bute Ministry in England, he attacked hypocrisy and corruption in a manner Forster found moral, positive, and timeless. In his poem *Conference,* he even attempted instruction by providing negative details of his own life and expressing remorse in a discussion of the pangs of a guilty conscience.

Here, then, was a man who at last found in letters a profession able to offer him dignity and financial security, a chance to benefit his fellowmen, and the opportunity, in part, to exorcise his own personal failings. Taken all in all, Forster argued—and he included Churchill's works, his personal life, and the values of his age in making the appraisal—Churchill must be seen as worthy of at least a minor place at table with the masters. Forster is unequivocal on that point:

. . . . it is not by the indifferent qualities in his works that Charles Churchill should be judged, and, as he has too frequently been, condemned. Judge him at his best; judge him by the men whom he followed in this kind of composition; and his claim to the respectful and enduring attention of the students of English poetry and literature, becomes manifest. Of the gross indecencies he has none. . . . There was not a form of mean pretence, or servile assumption, which he did not denounce. Low, pimping politics, he abhorred: and that their vile abbetors, to whose exposure his works are so incessantly devoted, have not carried him into utter oblivion with themselves, sufficiently argues for the sound morality and permanent truth expressed in his manly verse. ("Churchill," 247)

The biographies of Defoe and Steele, like those of Foote and Churchill, show Forster concerned with each writer's reputation, but with significant differences. Of course neither Defoe nor Steele had lapsed into the obscurity of Churchill or Foote. Forster's objective in the study of Defoe was to solicit for him a place in English letters appropriate to the full range of his achievements: "It is with De Foe dead, as it was with De Foe living. He stands apart from the circle of reigning wits of his time, and his name is not called over with theirs" ("De Foe," 1). In Steele's case, the judgment of his contemporaries and of posterity up to Forster's time was not the issue but rather his future literary reputation then threatened by the enormous prestige of Thomas Babington Macaulay, whose *The Life and Writings of Addison* had strengthened to a substantial extent claims for the greatness of Addison by invidious comparisons with Steele: "A magnificent eulogy of Addison is here built upon a most contemptuous depreciation of Steele; and if we are content to accept without appeal the judgment of Mr. Macaulay's Essay, there is one pleasant face the less in our Walhalla of British Worthies" ("Steele," 106).

Particularly emphasized in the study of Defoe are his independence of thought and his personal integrity with respect to matters of principle. His writings included virtually every type published during this period. And in his efforts to survive as an author, Defoe encountered every conceivable rebuff, including censorship, imprisonment, disagreements with publishers and booksellers, and literary piracy due to the lack of an adequate copyright law. Forster, who most fully detailed in his life of Goldsmith the struggle for dignity through authorship in the eighteenth century, said of Defoe: He is "our only famous politician and man of letters, who represented, in its inflexible constancy, sturdy dogged resolution, unwearied perseverence, and obstinate contempt of danger and of tyranny, the great Middle-class English character" ("De Foe," 90). Without doubt, Forster sympathized with most of Defoe's political and social views and was strongly attracted by the indomitable spirit Defoe demonstrated in standing up for principle regardless of the appeals of party even "through the thickest stir of the conflicts of the four most violent party reigns in English history" ("De Foe," 90).

Forster believed that this unshakable defense of political position exemplified genuine heroism, most particularly in that Defoe spoke unequivocally for the political ideals he supported even when knowing that the two specific groups he most wished to further were very likely to misunderstand his efforts. Indeed, the dissenters and the Whigs, in whose causes he toiled repeatedly, were each responsible for his two terms in prison. In the first instance, the dissenters failed to understand his defense of them against bigotry in *The Shortest Way with the Dissenters;* in the second instance, Defoe published three ironic pamphlets, urging that the Pretender be returned to the English throne upon the death of Queen Anne. Again his irony was completely unapprehended by many, including a certain "Whig light" whose "dulness" resulted in Defoe's being clapped into Newgate for a second time. A less immediately dangerous political pamphlet, though one still being debated even in Forster's time, was Defoe's *Letter* defending "popular representation," which Forster declared "remains still, as it was when first written, the most able, plain, and courageous exposition in our language, of the doctrine on which our own and all free political constitutions rest" ("De Foe," 37 n. 1).

As posterity had failed to appreciate Defoe's independent thinking and personal integrity regarding political principle, so it had ignored his genius for proposing sound measures for improving the social lot of the English citizenry. His *Essay on Projects* contained soundly reasoned suggestions touching virtually all aspects of life, including the education of women, the formal study of language, abolition of impressment, banking reform, improvement of roads, care for lunatics, and juster dealing with bankrupts and debtors. His greatest single vehicle, or "homely weapon" as Forster termed it, for disseminating his social and moral ideas was his journal *Review,* which he published three times a week for the nine years 1704–1713, regardless of whether he was at home, in jail, out of the country, in hiding from the bailiffs—however incommoded.

Forster felt little need to speak as advocate, though his remarks were both superlative and categorical, for "immortal" Defoe, the writer of fiction. The "secret" of the "fascination" of *Robinson Crusoe, Moll Flanders, History of the Plague, Roxanna,* and *Colonel Jack* was their "Reality. . . . The art of natural story-telling, which can discard every resort to mere writing or reflection, and rest solely on what people, in peculiar situations, say and do, just as if there were no reader to hear all about it, has had not such astonishing illustrations" ("De Foe," 96). Forster, indeed, offered Defoe the highest accolade: after noting that *Crusoe* and *Moll* have never been surpassed, he hung upon Defoe the epithet "father of the illustrious family of the English Novel" ("De Foe," 97) and traced in novelists to his own day their debt to this "father."

Forster's defense of Steele is, in effect, a *vade mecum* of his theories of literary biography. The task with Steele was hindered, as Forster clearly recognized, by having to offset the judgment of so well known an essayist and historian as Lord Macaulay. As a result, Forster spent literally half of this hundred-page study refuting Macaulay, thereby blurring somewhat the biographical focus of his work. Nevertheless, in the opening fifty pages, we find him repeatedly defining his philosophy of character, in effect describing what we have observed in his other studies. It is true that Steele may have had a penchant for drink and debt, but in Forster's final assessment Steele's life had been "at least the life of a disinterested politician and patriot, of a tender husband, of an attached father, of a scholar, a wit, a man of genius, a gentleman" ("Steele," 115).

Forster described his biographical method in his opening remarks on Steele, saying that he would proceed not "without partiality" but also "not without frank and full allowance for the portion of evil which is inseparable from all that is good, and for the something of littleness mixed up with all that is great" ("Steele," 106). But Forster was quick to point out what Steele himself had reminded his readers of in one of his "charming essays": "The word *imperfection* should never carry to the considerate man's heart a thought unkinder than the word *humanity* . . ." ("Steele," 106). Similarly, while still dealing with the personal weaknesses of Steele's character, Forster quoted approvingly a remark made by Bickerstaff: "The heathen world . . . had so little notion that perfection was to be expected from men, that among them any one quality or endowment in a heroic degree made a god. Hercules had strength, but it was never objected to him that he wanted wit. Apollo presided over wit, and it was never asked whether he had strength" ("Steele," 114). The modern age, of course, lacks the ancient capacity to tolerate heroes, and, Forster observed, comforts itself for its littleness by cutting great men down to size; speaking of Steele's wit and genius, he concluded that "the world, not content that their exercise should have enlarged the circle of its enjoyments, and added enormously to human happiness in various ways, must satisfy its vulgar eagerness to find feet of clay for its image of gold, and give censorious fools the comfort of speaking as ill as may be of their benefactor" ("Steele," 115).

To some extent Forster defended Steele's life by quoting from his letters, which show his devotion to his wife, and by quoting Steele's contemporaries: Pope, Swift, Young, Lady Montagu, and, of course, Addison himself. But Forster's "brief" depended principally upon Steele's essays—the only record Forster believed really mattered because the essays captured Steele's essential and best self, the self that would endure. By quoting at length from a broad sampling of *Tatler* numbers written before Steele's association with Addison as well as his later writing after that partnership began, Forster was able amply to demonstrate Steele's originality and his numerous accomplishments in the periodical essay. He points to the judgment of the reading public: Steele's essays have always been considered witty, moral, positive correctives for the manners and morals of his age.

While the literary defense was the most important, Forster also employed a rhetorical strategy. He consistently and strenuously objected to Macaulay's method of comparing Steele with Addison. Forster avoided all such comparisons and made much of doing so, concentrating wholly upon Steele's accomplishments and his ability to rest his literary reputation on the strength of these achievements. In this way, Forster seriously weakened Macaulay's position and suggested, at least implicitly, that perhaps Steele was the greater man.

To conclude discussion of the biographical sketches, we may briefly consider a few important likenesses between Defoe and Steele. In the creation of his *Review,* Defoe gave new form to periodical journalism and provided the model for Steele's *Tatler* and, later, for the *Spectator* of Steele and Addison. As Forster said, what Defoe did for the "citizen classes," the latter two did for the "beauties and the wits" ("De Foe," 57). The essays in these three journals ranged broadly over the mores of the day, preaching middle-class morality. These writers touched upon the moral and ethical dimensions of one particular issue we know to have been central to much of Forster's own thinking and writing in the 1840s and 1850s and to his vision of the men of letters whose lives he recorded: the trials of authorship specifically as they relate to legal protection of the writer's product.

Defoe's works were repeatedly the victims of literary piracy and mutilation. The law of this time guaranteed perpetual copyright to the author but had no mechanism for enforcement; as a result, as Defoe said, "no author is now capable of preserving the purity of his style, no, nor the native product of his thoughts, to posterity; since after the first edition of his work has shown itself . . . piratic printers or hackney abridgers fill the world, the first with spurious and incorrect copies, and the latter with imperfect and absurd representations, both in fact, style, and design" ("De Foe," 53 n). And Steele more than once took up the same note, "lamenting that a liberal education should be the only one which a polite nation makes unprofitable." Forster's familiar position is reiterated in his summary of Steele's remarks:

. . . how expensive is the voyage which is undertaken in the search of knowledge; how few there are who take in any considerable merchandise; how fewer still are those able to turn what they have so gained into profit; and then he asks the question, which it is the disgrace of two subsequent centuries to have left still imperfectly answered, whether it is not "hard, indeed, that the very small number who are distinguished with abilities to know how to vend their wares, and have good fortune to bring them into port, should suffer plunder by privateers under the very canon that should protect them?" ("Steele," 151)

The dignity, rights, and privileges of professional authorship constitute a recurrent theme in all of Forster's literary work. Yet nowhere was he to make the case in fuller detail or with greater persuasiveness than in his life of Goldsmith.

Oliver Goldsmith

The Life and Adventures of Oliver Goldsmith appeared in 1848, a handsome volume of seven hundred gilt-edged pages containing thirty-five illustrations by well-known artists such as Maclise, Stanfield, Leech, and Doyle. Its critical and popular approval encouraged Forster to spend the next six years revising and expanding it for a second edition, featuring numerous and extensive notes, entitled *The Life and Times of Oliver Goldsmith* (1854); this two-volume version, some three hundred pages longer than the original, enjoyed six reprintings in his lifetime.

In both private correspondence and published reviews, Forster received superlative praise for the earlier volume. Carlyle offered: "It is capital, equally good to the end. . . . Except *Boswell's* there is no biography in the English language worth naming beside it."[7] Dickens wrote that he had feared in the early part that Forster might be going to champion Goldsmith indiscriminately, "but I very soon got over that fear, and found reason in every page to admire the sense, calmness, and moderation, with which you make the love and admiration of the reader cluster about him: grow with his growth, and strengthen with his strength—and weaknesses too, which is better still."[8] Both men especially valued Forster's description of Goldsmith as a man of letters struggling for recognition, not to mention a decent living, in a time most unpropitious to professional authors. For Dickens, the "gratitude of every man who is content to rest his station and claims quietly on Literature and to make no feint of living by anything else, is your due for evermore."[9] In what was surely the highest praise and the most moving, Dickens wrote the words that Forster later proved never to have forgotten: "My dear Forster, I cannot sufficiently say how proud I am of what you have done. . . . I desire no better for my fame, when my personal dustyness shall be past the controul of my love of order, than such a biographer and such a Critic."[10]

Critical acclaim was not limited to the private remarks of close friends. An anonymous review in the *Athenaeum* was followed by De Quincey's twenty-five-page review essay in the *North British Review* and thirty-three pages in the *Edinburgh Review* by Edward Bulwer. The *Athenaeum* began categorically: "This is a real biography—on a new, and to our thinking good, principle," giving with the "ease and simplicity of fiction the known incidents . . . in the life of a really English worthy."[11] De Quincey, too, highly touted the volume: "This book accomplishes a retribution which the world has waited for through seventy and odd years. Welcome at any rate by its purpose, it is trebly welcome for its execution."[12] Bulwer first enumerated Forster's credentials, saying, "We know of no man more fit for the task . . . than Mr. Forster. He brings to it a mind habitually critical, subtle, and inquiring; that strong sympathy with men of letters which the life of Goldsmith especially demands; a large practical knowledge of the infirmities and misfortunes, as well as the virtues and solaces of the class, with which kindred pursuits must have made him familiar."[13] Bulwer, too, honored the execution: "a discriminating and intellectual biography. . . .—a gentle but manly apology for the life, which it tracks through each pathetic transition of light and shadow; written in that spirit of which Goldsmith himself would have approved—

pleasing while it instructs us, mild without tameness, earnest without acerbity."[14]

Forster sounded the theme of his study in the dedicatory sonnet to Dickens, a "fellow Goldsmithian": "Genius and its rewards are briefly told: / A liberal nature and a niggard doom, / A difficult journey to a splendid tomb."[15] Indeed, Forster achieved two distinct but related purposes in this *Life:* to record the specific biography of Oliver Goldsmith (1728–1774), hero-as-man-of-letters who produced such delightfully instructive and entertaining works as *Letters from a Citizen of the World, The Vicar of Wakefield, The Deserted Village,* and *She Stoops to Conquer,* in addition to many wonderful essays; and to show the plight of the typical man of letters trying to find dignity and reward in an era when the grand patron was gone and the professional writer toiled at the mercy of the often mercenary and sometimes unscrupulous bookseller.

Forster divided his presentation into four books. In each we witness Goldsmith's weaknesses and mistakes spread upon a broad canvas, but also in each we come to share Forster's mitigating assessment of these flaws as he emphasizes Goldsmith's good heart, explains away his painful social ineptness, and chastises those who knew and appreciated him best—Johnson, Reynolds, Burke—for the lack of feeling they too often demonstrated toward him. And, as always, problematic biographical details are put into perspective by the reader's never being long away from discussion of Goldsmith's literary genius as revealed in the major works he created.

Goldsmith's first thirty years constituted a virtually unbroken series of misadventures. He drifted aimlessly, suffering through young childhood—where he was considered "impenetrably stupid" (*Goldsmith,* 3)—desultory schooling, physical abuse from his tutor at college, and failure to find a suitable profession despite efforts toward religion, education, law, and medicine. But, constant in all of the aimlessness, idleness, and eternal indebtedness, Goldsmith maintained a gentle cheerfulness, an unstinting charity toward those with less than he, and a sometimes very touching humanity, such as in the scenes of his playing the flute for his keep as he wandered across Europe. Speaking of these times, especially of two years of almost total idleness, Forster urged that the reader not judge negatively—as the world too quickly does—this soon to be hero-as-man-of-letters, for he will turn to good account even his genuine frailties:

. . . if these irregular early years unsettled him for the pursuits his friends would have had him follow, and sent him wandering, with no pursuit, to mix among the poor and happy of other lands, he assuredly brought back some secrets both of poverty and happiness which were worth the finding, and, having paid for his errors by infinite personal privation, turned all the rest to the comfort and instruction of the world. There is a Providence that shapes our ends, rough-hew them how we will; and to charming issues did the providence of Goldsmith's genius shape these rough-hewn times. . . . . Through the pains and obstructions of his childhood, through the uneasy failures of his youth, through the desperate struggles of his manhood, it lighted him to those last uses of experience and suffering which have given him an immortal name. (*Goldsmith*, 30–31)

These lines offer a schema for the entire volume: Forster detailed Goldsmith's "pains," "obstructions," "desperate struggles," and "suffering"; he then discussed their meanings by showing them transmogrified into various of Goldsmith's works. As we have seen in Forster's biographies of other writers, such works reveal the artist's moral nature and show the value for mankind of what that moral nature communicated in the author's best writing. At the same time, we witness an heroic spirit in its struggle to create in the grossly unfavorable Grub Street world of the mid-eighteenth century.

Book Two, "Authorship by Compulsion," and Book Three, "Authorship by Choice," are more similar in the events they relate than their titles suggest. In the first, we see clearly and painfully life as a Grub Street drudge; paid little for their efforts, authors must produce reams of work just to scrape by. To make matters worse, many hacks prostituted their pens for corrupt politicians, thereby giving all men of letters, by simple association, a disreputable social position: "To become author, was to be treated as adventurer: a man had only to write, to be classed with what Johnson calls the lowest of all human beings, the scribbler for party" (*Goldsmith*, 71–72). In Book Two, Goldsmith is shown busy at his new literary trade: writing reviews for the *Monthly Review*, where the publisher, Griffiths, added insult to low pay by allowing his wife to alter Goldsmith's copy; translating under a pseudonym; trying to write his own first work, "An Enquiry into the Present State of Polite Learning in Europe," also to be published without his name; and suffering incredible deprivation: "Oh Gods! Gods! HERE IN A GARRET,

WRITING FOR BREAD, AND EXPECTING TO BE DUNNED FOR A MILK SCORE!" (*Goldsmith,* 119).

Book Three reveals Goldsmith finally achieving success through *The Vicar of Wakefield* and *Letters from a Citizen of the World.* But the real change came in his growing relationship with Johnson, Reynolds, and Burke, who became Goldsmith's friends, particularly Johnson, who became a mentor of sorts. In Books Three and Four, the scenes among these men account for much of the volume's charm. They include, for example, the wonderful description of Boswell when Goldsmith first met him: "But little does Goldsmith or any other man suspect as yet, that within this wine-bibbing, tavern babbler, this meddling, conceited, inquisitive, loquacious lion hunter, this bloated and vain young Scot, lie qualities of reverence, real insight, quick observation, and marvelous memory, which, strangely assorted as they are with those other meaner habits, and parasitical, self-complacent absurdities, will one day connect his name eternally with the men of genius of his time, and enable him to influence posterity in its judgments on them" (*Goldsmith,* 259). But despite Goldsmith's fame and his friendships with many of the major figures of his age, life was filled with the old frustrations, interminable drudge labor for booksellers merely to keep himself out of debt, and the new frustration of struggling with Garrick in a first attempt to write and stage a comedy.

Also in Books Three and Four, Forster most directly confronted the common charges, both of Goldsmith's contemporaries and of posterity, that he was envious or jealous of the success of others and that he was so socially inept that he was a constant target for jokes and, occasionally, for more serious ridicule even among his friends and close acquaintances. Forster's rhetorical strategy for dealing with such allegations conformed to that pattern seen before in his literary biographies: he explained how these weaknesses occurred, making them appear at least understandable and, more often, entirely forgivable; he reduced their biographical significance by showing how they were apotheosized as exampla in Goldsmith's writings or were unimportant when juxtaposed with the author's essential character as revealed in his best works. For example, in one of the many instances where Forster asked the reader "charitably [to] judge" Goldsmith, he exhorted: "Nor let us omit from . . . consideration the nature to which he was born, the land in which he was raised, his tender temperament neglected in early youth, the brogue and the blunders he described as his only inheritance. . . . Manful, in spite of all, was Goldsmith's endeavor and noble its result" (*Goldsmith*, 445–46).

Such judgmental summaries of biographical facts are sprinkled heavily throughout this study. "Conversation is a game," Forster reminded his reader, referring to the numerous anecdotes describing Goldsmith's failures in polite gatherings, "where the wise do not always win. When men talk together, the acute man will count higher than the subtle man" (*Goldsmith*, 440). And of his envy or jealousy: "No one who thus examines the whole case can doubt, I think, that Goldsmith had never cause to be really content with his position among the men of his time. . . . even the booksellers who crowded round the author of *The Vicar of Wakefield* and the *Traveller*, came to talk but of booksellers' drudgery and catchpenny compilations. . . . May it not be forgiven him if, in galling moments of slighting disregard, he made occasional silent comparisons of *Rasselas* with the *Vicar*, of the *Rambler* with the *Citizen of the World* . . ." (*Goldsmith*, 441–42).

Hence in both his personal and his professional endeavors, Goldsmith suffered calamities: "But they found him, and left him, gentle; and though the discipline that taught him charity had little contributed to his social ease, by unfeigned sincerity and unaffected simplicity of heart he diffused every social enjoyment. When his conduct least agreed with his writings, these characteristics failed him not" (*Goldsmith*, ix–x). The *Goldsmith* volumes constitute Forster's last completed biography of eighteenth-century writers. The lives of Landor and Dickens presented their biographer very different problems, and despite obvious similarities, very different kinds of biographies resulted.

Walter Savage Landor

When Walter Savage Landor died at nearly ninety years of age in 1864, Forster had known him for almost thirty years and held copyright to all of his works, whose publication he had been superintending since the late 1830s; he had agreed as early as 1853 to be his official biographer. The task of writing his "life," however, must have appeared distinctly unappealing. For one thing, Forster was enormously busy: with the Lunacy Commission and with his return to the figures of his historical biographies of the 1830s, studies that he had begun to expand. More forbidding for the now eminent Victorian was the character and personality of Landor himself. Here was no hero-as-man-of-letters struggling against great odds to earn dignity and respect while creating instructive and entertaining literature for the middle class. Here, instead, was a man who wrote only to please himself, who gave away most of the money his writings produced, who cared little for his popularity as a writer, and whose works demanded such knowledge of classical and European history, languages, and literature that they were accessible only to the very few.

Appreciation of Landor's literary genius was further hindered by the same lack of discipline and restraint in his art as characterized all aspects of his personal life: born to enormous wealth, he lost or gave away most of it by early manhood; an impetuous collegian, he was forced to leave Oxford for firing a fowling piece into the occupied room of a fellow student whom he detested for his Tory leanings; as a young man he enjoyed and recorded in verse a series of amours and may have fathered an illegitimate child; nearly sixty years of age, he abandoned in Italy, personally but not financially, his wife and three children; and at eighty-three, he was driven from England into virtual exile to avoid costs from a scandalous libel case involving, among others, a sixteen-year-old girl. Throughout his life, although he was a stalwart liberal, generous to those who were in any way oppressed, and intimate with many of the most famous writers of his time, he fought constantly with friends, tenants, neighbors, publishers, and critics. And not a few of these violent outbursts and actions were public knowledge.

Additional complications existed in preparing the biography: Forster had not known Landor until the author was sixty-one years old, and he had to depend on Landor's brother Robert for much information about the writer's earlier days; many of Landor's friends and enemies were still alive, creating for a too-frank biographer problems as serious as possible libel. Hence, despite having at his disposal a vast collection of written materials, Forster faced a genuinely unpalatable task with this "life," one that threatened his integrity as a biographer and precluded the kind of biography of literary figures he most cherished: one that allowed him to argue unequivocally for the dignity of the profession of authorship and the importance to posterity of recovering and justly appreciating the works and essential character of writers he considered worthy of the highest public esteem. That he struggled with this venture is in part obvious by the fact that it took him five years to complete. That he was less than wholly successful is equally obvious upon examination of the resulting eleven-hundred-page, two-volume product, *Walter Savage Landor: A Biography* (1869).

Many features of this study are praiseworthy. The volumes contain upward of four hundred letters, most new to print. The single greatest treasure is the correspondence between Landor and Robert Southey, which records in detail a friendship of more than three decades between these two literary figures. Appearing, too, are certain of Landor's works never before published, including the last five scenes of his *Imaginary Conversations*. Generous extracts of Landor's writing abound, underpinned by equally generous portions of Forster's critical commentary, frequently lifted whole from the many reviews of Landor he had published in the *Examiner* and the quarterlies. One of the most serious weaknesses in the study, however, is that this material is inadequately assimilated, marring the coherence of the story. A modern critic has observed of this problem: "Forster . . . jumbled together the rich and abundant materials at his disposal in hodgepodge fashion apt rather to perplex than enlighten any serious reader. Dates are conspicuously absent from extracts of letters, which are employed in any manner that happened to suit the editor's convenience."[16] Nor was this central defect ignored by contemporary readers. Forster's friend Percy Fitzgerald sharply criticized the volumes for flaws in basic technique: "Forster dealt with him in his magisterial way, and furnished a heavy treatise, on critical and historical principles. Everything here is treated according to the strict canons and in judicial fashion. On every poem there was a long and profound criticism of many pages, which I believe was one of his own old essays used again, fitted into the book. The hero is treated as though he were some important historical personage."[17]

The distancing suggested by the phrase "historical personage" is both accurate and no doubt intentional. Forster wished to avoid suggesting too intimate a personal relationship with Landor. By far the most important contemporary praise for the volumes shows that this "distancing" was judged generally to have been effective and is precisely the praise that must at first strike a modern reader as most surprising: that the volumes are "frank," "candid," and "fair" in assessing Landor's character.

The *Examiner* raised this point directly, saying that a reader "will find the vague misrepresentations and guesses that have hitherto hung about the interpretations of Savage Landor's life and character dispelled by a clear, accurate, and remarkably frank narrative, in which one is no less struck by the largeness and interest of the theme than by the courage and honesty of the narrator."[18] Edward Dowden in the *Fortnightly Review* found acceptable some suppression of incidents in Landor's life, since, generally speaking, Landor could honestly be described as "emphatically an *uncivilised* man"; but more important was Dowden's support for the "truth" of Forster's portrait; he describes as fundamental to Forster's technique almost exactly that vision of "truth" (purposeful suppression included) that we have found in each of the literary biographies: "The information his book supplies is full, precise, and trustworthy; great pains have been taken to make the presentation of characters complete; there is no approach to tampering with facts through an unwise zeal of friendship; the biographer, allowance being made for some necessary reserves, before all else has striven to be truthful, and because entirely just, he has felt that in treating of such a man as Landor generosity is a part of justice."[19] Monckton Milnes in the *Edinburgh* linked the categorical tone of the *Examiner* with the breadth of Dowden's remarks: "Nothing is concealed that is worth revealing, nothing is lauded which is unjust, and nothing is left unreproved and unregretted which is wrong in moral conception or unbecoming in the action of life."[20]

To understand the extent to which this homage to Forster's candor is accurate, we need only to look at a few remarks from one of the negative reviews, in this instance one written by Eliza Lynn Linton, a close personal friend of Landor's who felt that his "eccentricities" were merely a part of his personal "style" and not a reflection of his essential character:

No book that we know of, save Hogg's reminiscenses of Shelley, can compare with it [Forster's] for the skill with which it has degraded and dwarfed its subject. We do not say that it is not truthful in fact, but it is not just in spirit. It has not created the small or ugly parts of Landor's character, but it has given them undue prominence . . . and so far it is untrue. . . . We will not say that it is intentionally false or unfair; but it is both in result; because . . . prominence is given to the evil and not to the good.[21]

Linton's criticism is keenly important: it underscores that Forster did genuinely attempt candor; it shows that in toning down his tendency to idealized portraits, the hallmark of his earlier literary biographies and surely the perspective that Linton most misses, Forster's sense of integrity as a biographer led him to a more absolute "truth" than he had accomplished earlier. Not that he completely abandoned all idealizing, for without doubt Forster felt compelled to make the best case he could for his longtime friend and unquestionably he genuinely believed that much in Landor's writings was worthy and reflected a unique genius, which the world had consistently and unfairly neglected. Here, of course, was precisely the difficulty: how to give Landor his due and remain truthful. One response to this problem was Forster's abandoning of the idea of "hero" when describing Landor. That word has little place in these volumes and is supplanted by "genius," "original," "unique," and "special" as positive terms. Further, Forster did not argue that Landor's character was essentially moral or that the excesses in his personal life were rendered unimportant by the value of his works. Indeed, he believed that Landor's self-centered and undisciplined life, often expressing itself in the lack of restraint in his writing, substantially reduced the stature of the man and of the writer. Recording this "truth" in the *Landor,* Forster remained consistent with his primary aesthetic principle—that the quality of the artistic vision is determined by the quality of the writer's essential character. The earlier writers whose lives he recorded appear as greater artists because the flaws in their personal lives were superficial, not fundamental aspects of their characters. Forster may have made errors in judgment about one or more of these earlier figures, but his firsthand knowledge of Landor's life precluded such errors in his case. Following out the truth of this principle in the *Landor,* Forster created a biography quite different from his earlier ones.

No single biographical fact, by itself, whether included, suppressed, or distorted in the *Landor,* reveals the difference: for example, Forster suppressed most of the details about Landor's early love affairs and his later scandal and court case—though that both occurred is indicated—in much the same way that earlier he suppressed details about the drunkenness, uncontrollable anger, and illegitimate children in the lives of Steele, Defoe, and Foote, respectively. But in the *Landor,* the biographer's candor, obvious from the outset, and the tone of his introductory remarks make clear that the negative judgments forthcoming about the writer's personal life possess greater importance than in the former studies:

> It is not my intention to speak otherwise than frankly of his character and his books. Though I place him in the first rank as a writer of English prose; though he was also a genuine poet. . . . It was unfortunate for him in his early years that self-control was not necessarily forced upon a temperament which had peculiar need of it; and its absence in later time affected both his books and his life disastrously. Even the ordinary influences and restraints of a professional writer were not known to him. Literature was to him neither a spiritual calling, as Wordsworth regarded it; nor the lucrative employment for which Scott valued it. Landor wrote without any other aim than to please himself, or satisfy the impulse as it rose. Writing was in that sense an indulgence to which no limits were put, and wherein no laws of government were admitted. (*Landor,* 1:2–3)

These lines, virtually the first set down, represent an almost exact reversal of Forster's usual emphases: heretofore the permanent value of the works—positive, instructive, and entertaining while reflecting the author's essentially moral character—has reduced the import of any personal failings noted. These opening lines do show, however, Forster's adherence to his most important critical principle: that the greatness of the art will correspond to the greatness of the artist's nature. Lack of restraint in the one, for example, should manifest itself in the other. In this sense, Landor provides an exact test of this principle. Had such an undisciplined nature produced works of ordered clarity, Forster would have been hard pressed to hold to his critical imperatives. But Landor's writing does lack discipline; the art and the man are of a piece. The difficulty came in saying so without seeming to betray a friend. Regardless, Forster meant every word of this initial judgment. Nearly eleven-hundred pages later, he wrote:

> What was wanting most, in his books and his life alike, was the submission to some kind of law. To this effect a remark was made at the opening of this biography, which has had confirmation in almost every page of it written since. . . . I am not going now to preach any homily over my old friend. Whatever there was to say has been said already with as much completeness as I found to be open to me. Attempt has been honestly made in this book to estimate with fairness and candour Landor's several writings . . . and judgment has been passed, with an equal desire to be

only just, on all the qualities of his temperament which affected necessarily not his own life only. . . . what was really imperishable in Landor's genius will not be treasured less, or less understood, for the more perfect knowledge of his character. (*Landor*, 2:593–94)

The emphasis in the present discussion upon the character of Landor fairly represents Forster's own proportioning. Although he offered critical analysis of Landor's writings, especially *Gebir, Count Julian,* and the *Imaginary Conversations,* through borrowings from his own critical reviews and especially from the letters of Southey, when he is speaking in his own voice of the late 1860s he usually hangs biographical detail upon his discussion of the literary works, frequently in the role of albatross. An example is Forster's assertion that the dialogue format is that most suited to Landor's talents and character: "When a man writes a dialogue he has it all to himself, the pro and the con, the argument and the reply. . . . In no other style of composition is a writer so free from orderly restraints upon opinion, or so absolved from self-control. . . . How far such a style or method would be found suitable to the weakness as well as the strength of the character depicted in these pages, the reader has the means of judging. By many it may be thought that I have supplied such means too amply" (*Landor*, 1:486–87).

Yet he ends his study with a fitting tribute to his friend wherein the life of this old firebrand political radical and the literary works he produced are seen in a worthy and admirable meld:

There is hardly a conceivable subject, in life or literature, which they [Landor's works] do not illustrate by striking aphorisms, by concise and profound observations, by wisdom ever applicable to the needs of men, and by wit as available for their enjoyment. Nor, above all, will there anywhere be found a more pervading passion for liberty, a fiercer hatred of the base, a wider sympathy with the wronged and the oppressed, or help more ready at all times for those who fight at odds and disadvantage against the powerful and the fortunate, than in the writings of WALTER SAVAGE LANDOR. (*Landor*, 2:595–96)

Forster did believe this judgment; yet much in the biography seriously erodes this positive final assessment. Without doubt the man Landor and Forster's *Landor* stand apart from the other writers and biographies Forster wrote. Landor is alone on a side track— "original," "individual," "unique" in his "genius"—but not a hero-as-man-of-letters in the line of writers from Defoe to Dickens whose "lives" constitute Forster's best and most coherent biographical writing.

Charles Dickens

When Charles Dickens died June 9, 1870, John Forster was best qualified to write the novelist's biography, and he was Dickens's own choice; praising Forster's *Goldsmith* in 1848, Dickens had concluded: "I desire no better for my fame when my personal dustyness shall be past the controul [*sic*] of my love of order, than such a biographer and such a Critic."[22] Dickens's willingness to share his most private thoughts is obvious in many of the nearly one thousand letters spanning an intimate relationship of thirty-three years that Forster quoted in *The Life of Charles Dickens;* indeed, it was to Forster that Dickens revealed his experience as a young boy in a blacking warehouse and the devastating effect it had on his self-image, the attendant relationship with his parents and others around him, and his childhood resolve for his future life. Dickens shared these details with no other person in his lifetime.

Whereas the biography of Landor presented Forster with serious problems, the greater part of Dickens's personal life and especially his works were excellent subjects for Forster, the advocate of the dignity of authorship as a profession. Dickens's works were universally acknowledged for their positive moral and social content; his own life, even apart from its Horatio Alger dimension, was full of public acts of charity that frequently included well-publicized efforts in company with Forster, Bulwer, and others to assist struggling authors. The weaknesses in Dickens's private life and character, such as his handling of the breakup of his marriage, could be seen simply as human failings, bringing Dickens the hero more properly into perspective as Dickens the human being, and not in any way genuinely contradictory to the positive moral bent of his essential character so well defined by his greatest works. Only Forster's health posed a serious impediment to the task of writing the *Life.* Davies's summary makes the point forcefully:

His health was appalling, his serious illnesses including rheumatic fever, rheumatism, bronchitis, gout, a liver complaint, skin diseases, and, in 1872, "frightful attacks of giddiness and sickness." He was "hurried and harried" on the asylum circuits of the Lunacy Commission, often traveling in dreadful weather. His last surviving sister died in 1869 and was followed by Dyce, Maclise, Fonblanque, Bulwer, and Macready. . . . . In December 1870 he wrote to Bulwer: "The Joy is gone out of my life—but I struggle on much as I can, with no certainty from day to day."[23]

The resulting three-volume study, *The Life of Charles Dickens* (1872–1874), was Forster's last completed work and clearly his crowning achievement. The format is similar to the *Landor:* much of the text is composed of Dickens's letters; a complete history of the writing and publishing details of each work is included with analyses of each novel, drawn in many cases from reviews published earlier. Unlike the *Landor,* the various biographical and critical details are handled in a unified and coherent style supporting Forster's opening descriptive judgment of Dickens, "the most popular novelist of the century, and one of the greatest humourists that England has produced" (*Life,* 1:3). The emphasis suggested in this opening is crucial: we have returned to a biography that describes the hero-as-man-of-letters.

The volumes were reviewed separately as they appeared. Positive assessments ranged from the matter-of-fact to Carlyle's unrestrained exuberance. The *Examiner,* speaking of the second volume, praised Forster's "exact appreciation of his friend's character . . . desire to tell the precise truth . . . vigour of delineation, growing out of his mastery of the literary art and of his thorough comprehension of Dickens's inner and outer life. . . ."[24] Whitwell Elwin said in the *Quarterly* that "it appears that a more faithful biography could not be written. . . . The real man is the Charles Dickens of Forster's biography."[25] Percy Fitzgerald, who had damned the *Landor* for its pompousness, found the *Dickens* much better: "Everything is . . . put together . . . with extraordinary art and finish. It furnishes a most truthful and accurate picture of the 'inimitable,' recognizable in every page."[26] Carlyle, who had been enthusiastic about the *Goldsmith,* declared, "you have given to every intelligent eye the power of looking down to the very bottom of Dickens's mode of existing in this world; and I say have performed a feat which, except in Boswell, the unique, I know not where to parallel. So long as Dickens is interesting to his fellow-men, here will be seen, face to face, what Dickens's manner of existing was. . . ."[27]

Negative criticism, of course, appeared also. The volumes were found wanting either because they seemed to reflect a too strong idealizing strain from an adulatory friend or because the character of Dickens was too much dwarfed by the "I" of his single correspondent. The *Saturday Review* took up the latter position at length: "The book should not be called the Life of Dickens but the History of Dickens's Relations to Mr. Forster. . . . It is the Johnson giving us the life of his Boswell. Dickens never takes a step in life, from the most trivial to the most important, without consulting his oracle; and whenever some rare accident leads him to neglect the oracle's advice, he generally has cause to repent."[28]

Forster took time in the third volume to respond to such criticism, specifically defining his intentions and justifying his technique:

Though Dickens bore outwardly so little of the impress of his writings, they formed the whole of that inner life which essentially constituted the man; and as in this respect he was actually, I have thought that his biography should endeavour to present him. The story of his books, therefore, at all stages of their progress, and of the hopes or designs connected with them, was my first care. With that view, and to give also to the memoir what was attainable of the value of such autobiography, letters to myself, such as were never addressed to any other of his correspondents, and covering all the important incidents in the life to be retraced, were used with few exceptions exclusively. (*Life,* 2:417–18)

Forster intended to make "Dickens the sole central figure in the scenes revived, narrator as well as principal actor" (*Life,* 2:418). The letters to himself, he asserted, served this end perfectly because

It is the peculiarity of few men to be to their most intimate friend neither more nor less than they are to themselves, but this was true of Dickens; and what kind or quality of nature such intercourse expressed in him, of what strength, tenderness, and delicacy susceptible, of what steady level warmth, of what daily unresting activity of intellect, of what unbroken continuity of kindly impulse through the change and vicissitude of three and thirty years, the letters to myself given in these volumes could alone express. (*Life,* 2:418)

Forster accepted as the essential Dickens the Dickens of the letters. In this way, his defense of using the letters also refutes the charge that his study idealizes Dickens. The issue of idealization is, of course, pertinent to all of Forster's biographies. And it is with the "dignity of literature" question that the idealizing tendency is most

demonstrable. Focusing upon it, we may consider how Forster ma-
nipulated his materials in portraying Dickens in these volumes.

Modern scholarship has gone far in examining Forster's various
uses of documentary material in the *Life*. The editors of the Pilgrim
Edition of *The Letters of Charles Dickens* have discovered that Forster
occasionally altered letters by rephrasing or rearranging to emphasize
his own importance in a particular decision or event, by changing
dates, by "improving" style, usually to the end of making Dickens
more appealing, by implying that letters written to others were, in
fact, written to him. The editors' conclusion, however, is precisely
what we have found in the other biographies: Forster "had his subject
remarkably in perspective. He was, moreover, concerned not simply
with public image . . . but with the truth, as he conceived it. The
Life contains numerous small distortions of fact, but paradoxically
these distortions were in the interest of a larger, or ideal, truth."[29]

Working with the critical commentary on Dickens's works included in the biography, Alec Brice has found that these analyses,
largely from the pages of the *Examiner*, include, without identifi-
cation, some critiques not written by Forster but by other critics,
for example, Hunt and Fonblanque. Forster's motivation was to
recapture for his reader as closely as possible the contemporary reaction to each work by using reviews and letters to re-create these
moments: his success at producing a single style and nearly faultless
coherence is genuinely remarkable. This technique, as Brice points
out, is similar to that of Boswell with Johnson and Lockhart with
Scott: the biographer manipulates primary materials to create a
portrait of the man true to his experience of him. As was the case
with the letters: "it should be becoming clear now, that Forster
took pains to create what he saw as the true picture of Dickens,
and of the contemporary reception of his works."[30]

How, then, does Dickens, hero-as-man-of-letters, appear in these
volumes? He emerges as no simple character but a complicated
literary man whose life became more and more tragic and limited
as he grew older. In the period from the 1830s to the mid-1850s,
Dickens the man and author is unmatched in sheer physical energy
and popularity. Forster shows him outmaneuvering fellow reporters,
inventing a shorthand system he put to good use, and creating moral
and positive novels and stories peopled by hundreds of memorable
characters; his private life is a blur of travel (the letters from America
are wonderful in their details), charitable works, and enormous social

gatherings. Experimentation leads generally to success in the Christmas books but failure in establishing a weekly journal, *Master Humphrey's Clock,* and in editing a daily newspaper, the *Daily News.* The 1850s open optimistically: after repeated failures to find a journalistic outlet for his energies and social concerns, he succeeds in finding the proper vehicle with the founding of *Household Words,* his popularity rises with *David Copperfield* and *Bleak House,* and amateur theatricals and the Guild of Literature and Art provide him a means for aiding struggling authors. Typical of this early period is Dickens's energy and excitement over the writing of *A Christmas Carol:* ". . . with what a strange mastery it seized him for itself, how he wept over it, and laughed, and wept again, and excited himself to an extraordinary degree, and how he walked thinking of it fifteen and twenty miles about the black streets of London, many and many a night after all sober folks had gone to bed" (*Life,* 1:298).

Typical, too, of these good times, as Forster viewed them, was the expression of Dickens's just and noble heart in the great social themes of his fiction. Of Dickens's first book, the *Sketches by Boz,* Forster noted "that subtle sense and mastery of feeling which gives to the reader's sympathies invariably right direction, and awakens consideration, tenderness and kindness precisely for those who most need such help" (*Life,* 1:65). And speaking of the period following the success of the *Carol:* "He was to try and convert Society, as he had converted Scrooge, by showing that its happiness rested on the same foundations as those of the individual, which are mercy and charity not less than justice. . . . to set class against class he never ceased to think as odious as he thought it righteous at all times to help each to a kindlier knowledge of the other" (*Life,* 1:352–53). In Venice with Dickens at this time, Forster heard the novelist express a specific vision of his life's work as a writer: " 'Ah,' he said to me, 'when I saw those places [in Venice], how I thought that to leave one's hand upon time, lastingly upon the time, with one tender touch for the mass of toiling people that nothing could obliterate, would be to lift oneself above the dust of all the Doges in their graves, and stand upon a giant's staircase that Samson could not overthrow!' In varying forms this ambition was in all his life" (*Life,* 1:353).

But behind the buoyant optimism, intense dedication to improved social justice, and extraordinary success of these years were darker intimations, which Forster also recorded. These judgments first

appear in the assessment of Dickens's blacking warehouse experience—where the young boy was humiliated by being taken from
school and forced to do drudge work pasting labels on jars of boot-
black while his family was for a brief period resident in the Mar-
shalsea debtor's prison. As a result of this trial, Dickens determined
never again to face poverty and social degradation. His success in
avoiding any similar experience when in control of his own fate
prompted, Forster believed, a "too great confidence in himself, a
sense that everything was possible to the will that would make it
so," and produced in him "something that had almost the tone of
fierceness; something in his nature that made his resolves insuper-
able, however hasty the opinions on which they had been formed"
(*Life*, 1:37). This assessment rendered very early in the first volume
contains Forster's explanation for the harmful decisions, both large
(separation from his wife, his public readings) and small (squabbles
with publishers, using real people as models for negative characters),
that Dickens made throughout his life. The tragic mistakes this
character flaw produced came in the later years of Dickens's life,
1858–1870.

Over the separation from his wife, Forster struggled to accord
Dickens justice. He quoted the author's letter on the incompatibility
of his and Catherine's personalities and particularly of his own rest-
lessness: "I have now no relief but in action. I am become incapable
of rest. . . . Why is it, that as with poor David, a sense comes
always crushing on me now, when I fall into low spirits, as of one
happiness I have missed in life, and one friend and companion I
have never made?" (*Life*, 2:217, 219). Forster could accept no ex-
cuse. He explained that Dickens had learned the value of a "determined resolve" from his early sufferings but nothing of "renunciation
and self-sacrifice"; more than that, his early rise to fame made him
"master of everything that might seem to be attainable in life, before
he had mastered what a man must undergo to be equal to its hardest
trials" (*Life*, 2:215). He concluded his brief discussion of the
breakup—one that never hinted of Dickens's affair with Ellen Ternan, an eighteen-year-old actress—with unequivocal condemnation
couched in the language of fairness: "Such illustration of grave
defects in Dickens's character as the passage in his life affords, I
have not shrunk from placing side by side with such excuses in
regard to it as he had unquestionable right to claim should be put
forward also" (*Life*, 2:229–30).

The public readings, unlike Dickens's relationship with his wife, touched directly on the literary side of his life, specifically for Forster, on the dignity-of-literature issue. For that reason he dealt with them prominently—nearly a fourth of the third volume is devoted to the readings. Forster's position was consistent and unequivocal: "It was a substitution of lower for higher aims; a change to commonplace from more elevated pursuits; and it had so much of the character of a public exhibition for money as to raise, in the question of respect for his calling as a writer, a question also of respect for himself as a gentleman" (*Life,* 2:222). The "dignity" issue so defined soon ceases to be the problem in that more serious consequences result from the readings than questions of social prestige. Forster links Dickens's desire to escape into the readings and into the applause of the crowd with Dickens's desire to escape the dissolution of his marriage, and Dickens's remarks about his motivations at this time—"Much better to die, doing" (*Life,* 2:218)—echoes ominously in the reader's mind as Forster piles up the correspondence from a Dickens exultant in the enormous amounts of money he is making and the effects he is creating on his tours both at home and in America. As we see Dickens relentlessly pursuing his readings despite severe physical breakdowns, involving paralysis in his foot, blurring of his vision and his speech, and various other problems, including giddiness and lightheadedness, we can see the accuracy of Davies's conclusion: "It seems odd to deny that Forster knew exactly what he was doing in the *Life,* when he . . . organized his documents to suggest that Dickens killed himself for money."[31]

The greatest single accomplishment of these volumes, beyond their giving to the world this unflinchingly three-dimensional portrait of Dickens, involves the dignity-of-literature issue and Forster's own place in the *Life.* It is Forster himself who carries the torch of hero-as-man-of-letters unremittingly throughout. This fact is not readily apparent and hence not intrusive for two reasons: in the years from 1837–1857, Forster and Dickens share the limelight: Forster as advisor, confidant, and companion assists Dickens in all his literary enterprises but in a dutifully subordinate role, always helping in very tangible ways but always willingly subordinate to the literary genius. After 1857–58, with Dickens's separation from his wife and the inception of the first reading tours, Forster was not much directly on the stage, but his judgments, particularly about the readings, hang over all of Dickens's obsessive concerns for money and approval as he quite literally drives himself to self-destruction, vindicating terribly Forster's original disapproval. In these two major crises, but also in a host of smaller ones—in disputes with his publishers; in opposing Dickens's decision to edit the *Daily News*, to publish a letter justifying his separation, to include the "Nancy-Sikes" reading; and by publishing Dickens's will wherein Ellen Ternan received the first bequest, £1,000—Forster upheld dignity in his own person and judged Dickens severely for its lack in him.

We see, then, that Forster captured the complexity of Dickens's character even as he affirmed characteristic moral judgments, particularly as they affect the dignity of literature as a profession. But while Forster saw Dickens as a complicated man, he also held a consistent vision of Dickens's essential self. Forster was grieved by what he described as the tragedy of Dickens's later years, but his tone is never harsh, only sad. Forster himself never lost sight of what was noble in Dickens's character; the closing scenes and the reaction of the world after his death are genuinely affecting. Forster revered Charles Dickens, and the greatness bodied forth in his best works, forming "the whole of that inner life which essentially constituted the man," went far in Forster's vision of this literary genius to mitigate the sad confusions evident in certain of his actions in the later years.

Chapter Five
Hero-as-Man-of-Letters

It is incredible, surely, that one man could possess so many qualities in common with men as different as Johnson, Boswell, and Podsnap. Yet John Forster was like Johnson: ". . . the same social intolerance; the same 'dispersion of humbug'; the same loud voice, attuned to a mellifluous softness on occasion, especially with ladies or persons of rank; the love of talk in which he assumed the lead—and kept it too; and the contemptuous scorn of what he did not approve";[1] he was like Boswell: intimate with Dickens for more than three decades, Forster was without rival in having access to the thoughts and words of that great literary genius of his day, and the comparisons to Boswell suggested by Carlyle and others after reading *The Life of Charles Dickens* further this view; and he was, in many moods, like Podsnap in Dickens's *Our Mutual Friend*—the perfect depiction of what was most offensive in Victorian middle-class complacency and national chauvinism—as is obvious in the following parody of Forster's concern with the dignity and respectability of literary men: "Mr. Podsnap, as a representative man, is not alone in caring very particularly for his own dignity, if not that of his acquaintances, and therefore in angrily supporting the acquaintances who have taken out his Permit, lest, in their being lessened, he should be."[2] After noting these personal similarities, however, we have made little headway in apprehending Forster's own genius and essential character; as he pointed out repeatedly in his criticism and literary biographies, that essential character is to be found principally in an author's works.

According Forster the just appraisal attendant to a reading of his best works is difficult: his critical reviews are buried in the files of the *Examiner* and other now-rare newspapers, and in the only slightly more often consulted quarterlies; his historical writings and, too, his biographies of eighteenth-century literary figures have been largely superseded; and his only widely known work, *The Life of Charles Dickens,* serves primarily as a reference tool for persons studying Dickens. Due, therefore, to Forster's too perfect, and frequently too

voluble, embodiment of Victorian middle-class respectability in his
personal life, the relative inaccessibility of some of his best writing
(his criticism), the datedness of much of the rest, and an interest
focused almost exclusively upon the subject and not upon the author
in his single work still well known today, his reputation as one of
the premier men of letters of his time is largely eclipsed. But just
as Esther Summerson in Dickens's *Bleak House* is not, despite superficial similarities, any of the persons whose names others give
her as nicknames—Dame Durden, Mother Hubbard, Little Old
Woman, Mother Shipton, Minerva—so Forster is not in any important essential a Johnson, Boswell, or Podsnap. The man revealed
in his writings and in the enduring personal actions of his life was
an intelligent, sensitive, extraordinarily helpful, just but ever-gen-
erous individual who left a very palpable imprint on many of the
major literary artists of his day.

Some of his finest work, if not always his most elegant prose,
considering the time constraints involved, is his criticism. His complete mastery of the tastes of his age, expanded and liberalized by
his own vast reading in classical literature and the English masters
of the sixteenth, seventeenth, and eighteenth centuries, allowed him
to note and record praise for virtually every contemporary writer
and dramatist we now consider worthy. Perhaps the worst that can
be said of his criticism is that he was "slightly inaudible about
Keats, Thackeray, and Emily Brontë," though "he did not fail to
record, in some measure, his recognition of excellence there," and
that he overpraised Bulwer as a dramatist and, possibly, Landor's
works.[3] The assistance he gave to men such as Browning, Bulwer,
Tennyson, Landor, Dickens, and Carlyle is incalculable because our
only records are letters and his formal critiques; the informal, oral
advice and criticism are, of course, lost, though obvious from the
recorded comments of these famous men themselves. Each privately
acknowledged the value to him personally of Forster's advice, and
all but Tennyson in this grouping did so publicly either by dedicating to him individual works or collected editions or by naming
him literary executor. More important than any assistance Forster's
reviews may have produced for individual works or reputations is
the extent to which his published criticism provides a comprehensive
gloss on the moral aesthetics of the cultivated, middle-class reader
of the early and high Victorian age regarding literary, political, and
religious ideas.

The histories and historical biographies offer essentially the same value, however much they may present a picture of the Commonwealth period now known to be partial. In them we find eloquently and forcefully expressed a Whig view centered to a large extent upon a Carlylean conception of the hero in history. In an accurate and not ungenerous assessment of these works, historian Samuel Gardiner noted: "He never attached himself to unworthy objects. . . . His portraits . . . have in them the life which springs from sympathy. From them the world learned, not quite all that Eliot and Pym and Hampden really were, but what they wished to be."[4]

Seeing in the figures of his literary biographies the same uncomprised integrity, the same indomitable commitment to their work, and the same moral center to their character that he saw in the patriots of the Commonwealth, Forster argued unequivocally for the dignity of the profession of authorship by underscoring the importance to posterity of justly appreciating the moral, positive, and entertaining works of writers he considered worthy of the highest public esteem. Throughout all of his writings and in his private life, he urged a more just evaluation of the profession of letters, believing it to be more valuable to the nation than those of business, law, or the military. In dedicating himself and his works to this struggle for a just recognition, respect, and reward for men of letters, he saw himself as a critic in company with Hazlitt, Lamb, and Hunt—and truly he was their heir.

As in the case with his hero, Dryden, "literature was his trade: he not only lived upon its wages, but was never afraid to own it."[5] Effecting in his own work the great middle-class characteristics he attributed to Defoe—"inflexible constancy, sturdy dogged resolution, and unwearied perseverance" ("De Foe," 90)—he transcended in his writing any of the negative characteristics in his personal life suggested by comparisons to Johnson, Boswell, or Podsnap. In his honest striving to recognize, encourage, and publicize both the best and the most promising writers of his own time and to record as exemplars the lives of particular literary geniuses, he assisted many to the reputations and rewards they deserved. Judged by his best writings, any negative personal characteristics are reduced to insignificance, and John Forster emerges as one with the writers he most cherished: a hero-as-man-of-letters.

Notes and References

Preface

1. Quoted in Malcolm Elwin, "John Forster," in *Victorian Wall-flowers* (London, 1934), pp. 178–79.
2. "History of the *Examiner,*" *Eclectic Magazine* 27 (October 1852):232.

Chapter One

1. Percy Fitzgerald, "John Forster: A Man of Letters of the Old School—A Reminiscence," *Month* 96 (July-December 1900):361.
2. R. C. Lehmann, *Memories of Half a Century* (London: Smith, Elder, 1908), p. 126.
3. [Percy Fitzgerald], *John Forster by One of His Friends* (London, 1903), p. 1.
4. *The Letters and Private Papers of William Makepeace Thackeray,* ed. Gordon N. Ray (Cambridge, Mass., 1945), 1:377.
5. *The Diaries of William Charles Macready 1833–1851,* ed. William Toynbee (London, 1912), 2:74.
6. Quoted in Elwin, "John Forster," pp. 178–79.
7. *Letters from Elizabeth Barrett to B. R. Haydon,* ed. Martha Hale Shackford (Oxford: Oxford University Press, 1939), p. 75.
8. *Jane Welsh Carlyle: A New Selection of Her Letters,* ed. Trudy Bliss (New York, 1950), p. 145.
9. *The Letters of Mrs Gaskell,* ed. J. A. V. Chapple and Arthur Pollard (Cambridge, Mass.: Harvard University Press, 1967), pp. 242–47, 280–81, 287–89, respectively.
10. *Diaries,* 1:262. See also Malcolm Elwin, "The Doctor," in *Victorian Wallflowers,* pp. 117–22, and "Laetitia Elizabeth Landon," *Dictionary of National Biography* (London, 1922), 11:493–94.
11. Letter to Georgina Hogarth, 3/11/1856, quoted in Edgar Johnson, *Charles Dickens: His Tragedy and Triumph* (New York, 1952), 2:857.
12. Arthur Waugh, *A Hundred Years of Publishing* (London: Chapman & Hall, 1930), p. 69.
13. Quoted in Elwin, "John Forster," p. 179.
14. [Fitzgerald], *John Forster,* p. 18.
15. William Lockey Harle, "John Forster: A Sketch," *Monthly Chronicle of North-Country Lore and Legend* 2 (February 1888):50. The most comprehensive coverage of Forster's life through the mid-1850s, focusing

principally on his journalism, is Sister Mary Callista Carr, "John Forster: A Literary Biography to 1856" (Ph.D. diss., Yale University, 1956). For discussions of Forster that are essentially reminiscences, see the two pieces by Fitzgerald already noted; R. H. Horne, "John Forster: His Early Life and Friendships," *Temple Bar* 46 (January-April 1876):491–505; Blanchard Jerrold, "John Forster," *Gentleman's Magazine*, n.s. 16 (January-June 1876):313–19; and Richard Renton, *John Forster and His Friendships* (London, 1912). For general surveys of Forster's life, see Whitwell Elwin, "John Forster," in the *Catalogue of Printed Books, Forster Collection* (London, 1888), pp. vii–xxvii; Harle, "John Forster," pp. 49–54; Charles Kent, "John Forster," *Dictionary of National Biography* (London, 1922), 7:456–59; and Henry Morley, "Biographical Sketch of Mr. Forster," in *Handbook of the Dyce and Forster Collections in the South Kensington Museum* (London, 1880), pp. 53–73. My discussion is most indebted to the sketches of Whitwell Elwin and Henry Morley, and to the fine study by Sister Mary Callista Carr.

16. Carr, "John Forster," pp. 2–3.

17. Quoted in Renton, *John Forster,* p. 8.

18. Carr, "John Forster," pp. 8–9.

19. Quoted in James A. Davies, "Leigh Hunt and John Forster," *Review of English Studies,* n.s. 19 (1968):25. See also pp. 25–40 and Elwin, *Catalogue of Printed Books,* pp. x–xi, for the importance of this friendship to each man.

20. Jerrold, "John Forster," pp. 315–16. The story in this version is that a cabman calling at the offices of the *Daily News* to pick up his fare could not describe the person to the porter's satisfaction until he said, "You know who I mean—I mean that there harbitrary cove." Armed with this description, the porter went directly to Forster. This nickname became a favorite of Forster's friends, and Fitzgerald notes Forster's using it on himself at least once, *John Forster,* p. 28.

21. See James A. Davies, "Charles Lamb, John Forster, and a Victorian Shakespeare," *Review of English Studies,* n.s. 26 (1975):442–50, and Carr, "John Forster," pp. 26–31, for full discussions of Lamb's influence on Forster.

22. Edgar Finley Shannon, Jr., *Tennyson and the Reviewers* (New York, 1967), p. 18. Shannon offers generous extracts of Forster's reviews of Tennyson.

23. *Diaries,* 1:36, n. 5.

24. November 26, 1837. See Carr, "John Forster," pp. 53–60, 68–70.

25. Ibid., pp. 84–86.

26. *Diaries,* 1:478.

27. *Bulwer and Macready: A Chronicle of the Early Victorian Theatre,* ed. Charles H. Shattuck (Urbana, Ill., 1958), p. 100.

28. Carr, "John Forster," pp. 141–42.

29. *Personal and Literary Letters of Robert, First Earl of Lytton,* ed. Betty Balfour (London: Longmans, Green, 1906), 1:346.

30. *Examiner,* September 6, 1835. Quoted in William Clyde DeVane, *A Browning Handbook* (New York: Appleton-Century-Crofts, 1955), p. 56.

31. *New Letters of Robert Browning,* ed. William Clyde DeVane and Kenneth Leslie Knickerbocker (New Haven, Conn., 1950), p. 230.

32. Ibid., pp. 72–73.

33. Ibid., pp. 137–40.

34. Lehmann, *Memories,* pp. 112–13.

35. Quoted in S. M. Ellis, *William Harrison Ainsworth and His Friends* (London, 1911), 1:323.

36. Elizabeth Johnston, "John Forster: Critic" (Ph.D. diss., University of Pittsburgh, 1947), p. 262.

37. See Philip Collins, "Dickens' Self-Estimate: Some New Evidence," in *Dickens the Craftsman: Strategies of Presentation,* ed. Robert B. Partlow, Jr. (Carbondale, 1970), pp. 21–43; for a differing point of view on this issue, see Alec W. Brice, "Reviewers of Dickens in the *Examiner:* Fonblanque, Forster, Hunt, and Morley," *Dickens Studies Newsletter* 3 (1972):68–80.

38. Waugh, *A Hundred Years,* p. 29.

39. Ibid., pp. 27–37, for Forster's help in securing Dickens's work for Chapman and Hall.

40. See DeVane, *A Browning Handbook,* pp. 62–69, and Bruce S. Busby, "A Note to the Editor of Thomas Wentworth, Earl of Strafford," *Studies in Browning and His Circle* 5 (1977):65–70.

41. Quoted in Renton, *John Forster,* p. 143.

42. Quoted in Ellis, *Ainsworth,* 2:56.

43. Charles Richard Sanders, "Carlyle's Letters," *Bulletin of the John Rylands Library* 38 (1955):223. Sanders offers a fine overview of the relationship between these two men as seen through Carlyle's letters.

44. James Anthony Froude, *Thomas Carlyle: A History of His Life in London 1834–1881* (London: Longmans, Green, 1919), 2:338.

45. Ibid., pp. 441–42.

46. Johnston, "John Forster," p. 3.

47. Kathleen Tillotson and Nina Burgis, "Forster's Reviews in the *Examiner,* 1840–1841," *Dickensian* 68 (1972):105.

48. Elwin, *Catalogue of Printed Books,* p. xiv.

49. See Carr, "John Forster," pp. 432–36, for details of Forster's attack on the American press and the controversy that ensued.

50. Ibid., pp. 448–49.

51. Ibid., p. 442; see pp. 439–42 for details of allegations by Prior.

52. Quoted in Rosalind Vallance, "Forster's *Goldsmith,*" *Dickensian* 71 (1975):24.

53. K. J. Fielding, "Thackeray and the Dignity of Literature," *TLS,* 19 September 1958, p. 536. This article, which continues, *TLS,* 26 September 1958, p. 552, is an excellent historical survey of the "dignity of literature" movement and the place in it of Bulwer, Dickens, Thackeray, and Forster. See also [K. J. Fielding?], "Dickens and the Royal Literary Fund," *TLS,* 15 October 1954, p. 664, and 22 October 1954, p. 680, on the same subject, focusing principally upon the efforts of the Guild of Literature and Art and the Royal Literary Fund.

54. See Carr, "John Forster," pp. 261–67, for the early relationship between Forster and Thackeray and Thackeray's contributions to the *Foreign Quarterly Review.*

55. *Letters and Private Papers of William Makepeace Thackeray,* 2:294–305.

56. Fielding, "Thackeray," p. 536.

57. Carr, "John Forster," p. 282.

58. Robert B. Martin, *Tennyson: The Unquiet Heart* (Oxford: Clarendon Press, 1980), p. 298; for full account of this unfortunate episode see pp. 295–98. See also Macready's *Diaries,* 2:322, 323–25, and John Bush Jones, "Tennyson, Forster, and the *Punch* Connection," *Victorian Periodicals Newsletter* 11 (1978):118–21.

59. *Tennyson, A Memoir,* ed. Hallam Tennyson (New York: Macmillan, 1906), p. 316.

60. Ibid., p. 326.

61. [Fielding?], "Dickens," p. 680.

62. Johnson, *Dickens,* 2:702, 856–57.

63. The phrase is Johnson's, *Dickens,* 2:905. See John Forster, *The Life of Charles Dickens,* ed. B. W. Matz (London: Chapman & Hall, 1911), 2:222–23.

64. Harle, "John Forster," p. 53.

65. Edward Barrington de Fonblanque, *The Life and Labours of Albany Fonblanque* (London: Richard Bentley & Son, 1874), p. 64.

66. Ibid., pp. 37–38.

67. Elwin, "John Forster," pp. 196–98.

68. Malcolm Elwin, *Landor: A Replevin* (London, 1958), pp. 19–20.

69. Carr, "John Forster," p. 222.

70. [Fitzgerald], *John Forster,* p. 64.

71. David Woolley, "Forster's *Swift,*" *Dickensian* 70 (1974):192.

72. "Mr. John Forster," *Athenaeum* 49 (January-June 1876):201.

73. Renton, *John Forster,* p. 269.

Chapter Two

1. This phrase was popularized by Isaac Disraeli and first used by him in the preface to *Calamities of Authors* (1812–13). Disraeli provided an important impetus for men like Bulwer, Dickens, and Forster to demand greater "dignity" or status for professional authors. In the 1840s and 1850s, this effort produced friction, particularly between Thackeray and Forster. For an excellent synthesis of the issues involved, see Fielding, "Thackeray and the Dignity of Literature," *TLS*, 19 September 1958, p. 536; 26 September 1958, p. 552.

2. "History of the *Examiner*," *Eclectic Magazine* 27 (October 1852):232.

3. For succinct surveys of the influence of Hunt and Lamb on Forster, see two articles by Davies, "Leigh Hunt and John Forster," pp. 25–40, and "Charles Lamb, John Forster, and a Victorian Shakespeare," pp. 442–50.

4. John Forster, "Charles Lamb: His Last Words on Coleridge," *New Monthly Magazine,* February 1835, p. 201.

5. Ibid.

6. "History of the *Examiner*," p. 232.

7. "The Claims of Authors to an Extension of Copyright," *Examiner,* April 7, 1839, p. 214.

8. Ibid., p. 215.

9. Ibid.

10. "International Copyright," *Examiner,* July 16, 1842, p. 453.

11. "The Literary Examiner," *Examiner,* January 17, 1846, p. 35.

12. Ibid.

13. Quoted in "The Dignity of Literature," *Examiner,* January 19, 1850, p. 35.

14. "Encouragement of Literature by the State," *Examiner,* January 5, 1850, p. 2.

15. Ibid.

16. Ibid.

17. "The Dignity of Literature," p. 35.

18. Ibid.

19. "Ill-Requited Services," *Examiner,* July 12, 1851, p. 433.

20. Ibid.

21. Ibid., p. 434.

22. Ibid.

23. "The Literary Examiner," *Examiner,* March 4, 1838, pp. 132–33.

24. "The Literary Examiner," *Examiner,* July 9, 1853, p. 435.

25. "Theatrical Examiner," *Examiner,* January 25, 1835, p. 52.

26. "Theatrical Examiner," *Examiner,* February 25, 1838, p. 118.

27. For a comprehensive overview of Forster's critical theories and practice, one to which this present discussion is much indebted, see Johnston, "John Forster," pp. 7–54, 70–124.

28. "The Literary Examiner," *Examiner*, November 1, 1835, p. 691.

29. "The Literary Examiner," *Examiner*, April 13, 1844, p. 227.

30. "The Literary Examiner," *Examiner*, November 13, 1836, p. 724.

31. "The Literary Examiner," *Examiner*, May 26, 1839, p. 324.

32. Ibid.

33. "The Literary Examiner," September 6, 1835, pp. 563–65, quoted in *Browning: The Critical Heritage*, eds. Boyd Litzinger and Donald Smalley (New York, 1970), p. 41. This collection of Browning criticism is particularly useful in allowing a reader to compare Forster's critical reaction with that of other critics reviewing Browning at the same time.

34. "Evidences of a New Genius for Dramatic Poetry.—No. I," *New Monthly Magazine*, March 1836, p. 290.

35. Ibid., p. 291.

36. "Theatrical Examiner," *Examiner*, May 7, 1837, p. 294.

37. Ibid.

38. *Browning: The Critical Heritage*, p. 6.

39. "The Literary Examiner," *Examiner*, October 2, 1841, pp. 628–29, quoted in *Browning: The Critical Heritage*, p. 71.

40. *Browning: The Critical Heritage*, p. 72.

41. "Theatrical Examiner," *Examiner*, April 2, 1842, pp. 232–34, quoted in *Browning: The Critical Heritage*, p. 79.

42. "The Literary Examiner," *Examiner*, November 26, 1842, p. 756–57, quoted in *Browning: The Critical Heritage*, p. 82.

43. "Theatrical Examiner," *Examiner*, February 18, 1843, p. 101, quoted in *Browning: The Critical Heritage*, p. 94.

44. "Theatrical Examiner," *Examiner*, June 22, 1844, pp. 388–89, quoted in *Browning: The Critical Heritage*, p. 102.

45. "The Literary Examiner," *Examiner*, November 15, 1845, pp. 723–24, quoted in *Browning: The Critical Heritage*, p. 104.

46. "The Literary Examiner, *Examiner*, April 6, 1850, pp. 211–13, quoted (with inaccurate dating) in *Browning: The Critical Heritage*, pp. 142–43.

47. "The Literary Examiner," *Examiner*, December 1, 1855, pp. 756–57, quoted in *Browning: The Critical Heritage*, pp. 162–63.

48. *Browning: The Critical Heritage*, p. 163.

49. "Literature," *True Sun*, January 19, 1833, quoted in Shannon, *Tennyson and the Reviewers*, p. 18. Shannon's discussions allow the reader to compare Forster's judgments with those of other contemporary critics.

50. "The Literary Examiner," *Examiner,* May 28, 1842, quoted in *Tennyson and the Reviewers,* p. 62.

51. "The Literary Examiner," *Examiner,* January 8, 1848, p. 21, quoted in *Tennyson and the Reviewers,* pp. 100, 115.

52. "The Literary Examiner," *Examiner,* June 8, 1850, quoted in *Tennyson and the Reviewers,* p. 142.

53. "The Literary Examiner," *Examiner,* August 4, 1855, p. 484.

54. An excellent exposition of Forster's critical aesthetic regarding fiction is K. J. Fielding's "Forster: Critic of Fiction," *Dickensian* 70 (1974):159–70.

55. *Life of Charles Dickens,* 1:96–97.

56. "The Literary Examiner," *Examiner,* November 18, 1838, p. 723.

57. "The Literary Examiner," *Examiner,* December 12, 1846, p. 788.

58. "The Literary Examiner," *Examiner,* November 3, 1839, p. 691.

59. "The Literary Examiner," *Examiner,* July 22, 1848, pp. 468–70, quoted in *Thackeray: The Critical Heritage,* eds. Geoffrey Tillotson and Donald Hawes (London, 1968), pp. 53, 54. This collection of Thackeray criticism allows a reader to compare Forster's critical commentary to that of other contemporary critics.

60. *Thackeray: The Critical Heritage,* p. 57.

61. "The Literary Examiner," *Examiner,* November 13, 1852, pp. 723–26, quoted in *Thackeray: The Critical Heritage,* pp. 146–47. It should be noted, in reference to the material on Thackeray extracted in the present discussion, that Forster regularly reviewed Thackeray's works throughout the 1840s and until 1855, and that he frequently described him as a "brilliant" writer and always found much to praise in his works, including *Vanity Fair* and *Henry Esmond.* But Forster objected repeatedly to Thackeray's misanthropy, his preference for caricature, and his tendency to "sneer." Not until *The Newcomes* (1855) does he find Thackeray willing to drop his former perspective on his characters and the world; the result is Forster's virtually unqualified praise of *The Newcomes* in "The Literary Examiner" for September 1, 1855.

62. For an excellent brief description of Forster's reaction to the generally undistinguished condition of the English stage as recorded in his "Theatrical Examiner" columns, see Johnston, "John Forster," pp. 286–93.

63. Full details of the influence of Lamb and Hunt on Forster's Shakespeare criticism may be found in Davies, "Charles Lamb, John Forster, and a Victorian Shakespeare," pp. 442–50.

64. "Theatrical Examiner," February 4, 1838, quoted in "Charles Lamb, John Forster, and a Victorian Shakespeare," p. 449.

65. *Dramatic Opinions and Essays* (New York: Brentano, 1906), 2:21, quoted in Johnston, "John Forster," p. 356.

66. "Theatrical Examiner," *Examiner,* August 24, 1834, p. 533.

67. "Theatrical Examiner," *Examiner,* October 23, 1836, p. 679.

68. "Theatrical Examiner," *Examiner,* November 6, 1836, pp. 711–12.

69. "Theatrical Examiner," *Examiner,* October 25, 1835, p. 677.

70. "Theatrical Examiner," *Examiner,* October 5, 1834, p. 629.

71. "Theatrical Examiner," *Examiner,* November 8, 1845, p. 709.

Chapter Three

Note: Unless otherwise indicated, quotations from Forster's works are drawn from the editions listed below and will be cited in the text by title (often shortened) and by page.

1. "Our Early Patriots," *Englishman's Magazine* 1 (April-August 1831):351–56; "John Pym," pp. 499–512; "Sir John Eliot," pp. 623–37; "Sir Henry Vane's Scheme of Parliamentary Reform," *Englishman's Magazine* 2 (Sept.-October 1831):1–13.

2. *Cabinet Cyclopaedia: Lives of Eminent British Statesmen,* ed. Dionysius Lardner (London, 1836–39), vols. 2, 3, 4, 6–7, respectively.

3. *The Statesmen of the Commonwealth of England; with a Treatise on the Popular Progress in English History* (London, 1840). References to this work will be to the American edition of John Overton Choules (New York: Harper, 1846).

4. *Diary and Correspondence of John Evelyn* (London: H. Colburn, 1850–52), 4 vols.

5. "The Civil Wars and Oliver Cromwell," *Edinburgh Review* 103 (January 1856):1–54.

6. *Historical and Biographical Essays* (London, 1858), 2 vols. References to these volumes will be to the facsimile edition (Westmead, Farnborough, Hants, England: Gregg International Publishers, 1972).

7. *Arrest of the Five Members by Charles the First* (London, 1860); *The Debates on the Grand Remonstrance, November and December,* 1641 (London, 1860).

8. *Sir John Eliot: A Biography* (London, 1864), 2 vols.

9. Samuel R. Gardiner, "Mr. John Forster," *Academy,* 5 February 1876, p. 122.

10. Edward Bulwer, "Arrest of the Five Members by Charles the First," *Quarterly Review* 108 (July-October 1860):499.

11. Ibid., 547.

12. "A History for Young England," *Jerrold's Shilling Magazine* 1 (1845):79, 80.

13. "Literary Examiner," *Examiner,* March 24, 1839.

14. *Sir John Eliot: A Biography,* 2d ed. (London: Chapman & Hall, 1872), n.p.

15. [Fitzgerald], *John Forster,* p. 9.

16. Bulwer, "Arrest," p. 499.

17. Throughout his historical writings in the 1830s, including his two-volume biography of Cromwell, Forster viewed the Lord Protector as a man who, despite an extraordinarily complex moral character, was finally to be judged a tyrant. Nevertheless, the mixture of good and evil in Cromwell's life, which Forster traced out in detail in the biographical volumes, proved sufficiently ambiguous to Forster when he considered it later that he could and did alter substantially his opinion in favor of Carlyle's assessment. With Carlyle's publication of *Oliver Cromwell's Letters and Speeches* (1845), Forster came to share, in the main, Carlyle's view of Cromwell as hero. Hence Forster's positive attitude toward Cromwell recorded in "The Civil Wars and Oliver Cromwell" in 1858 is much different from the negative one of the two-volume biography of 1838–39, which will be discussed later in this chapter.

18. "John Hampden," *New Monthly Magazine* 34 (February 1832):125.

Chapter Four

Note: Unless otherwise indicated, quotations from Forster's works are drawn from the editions listed below and will be cited in the text by title (often shortened) and by page.

1. "Charles Churchill," *Edinburgh Review* 81 (January 1845):46–88; "Daniel De Foe," *Edinburgh Review* 82 (October 1845):480–532; "Samuel Foote," *Quarterly Review* 95 (September 1854):483–548; "Richard Steele," *Quarterly Review* 96 (March 1855):509–68. These review essays were subsequently collected and reprinted with additions, principally fuller extracts from the writers' works and lengthy footnotes, as Volume 2 of Forster's *Historical and Biographical Essays.* All page citations in the text refer to the facsimile of the reprinted edition, Westmead, Farnborough, Hants, England: Gregg International Publishers, 1972.

2. *The Life and Adventures of Oliver Goldsmith* (London, 1848); *The Life of Jonathan Swift* (London, 1875), vol. 1.

3. *Walter Savage Landor: A Biography* (London, 1869), 2 vols.; *The Life of Charles Dickens* (London, 1872–1874), 3 vols. Page references in the text are cited from *The Life of Charles Dickens,* ed. B. W. Matz (London: Chapman & Hall, 1911), 2 vols.

4. James A. Davies, "Striving for Honesty: An Approach to Forster's *Life,*" *Dickens Studies Annual* 7 (1978):35.

5. "John Dryden and Jacob Tonson," *The Pic Nic Papers*, ed. Charles Dickens (London: H. Colburn, 1841), 1:55.

6. For a full discussion of Forster's essay on each of these men, see John Wilbert Braymer, "The Literary Biographies of John Forster" (Ph.D. diss., University of Tennessee, 1977), pp. 31–71.

7. *New Letters of Thomas Carlyle*, ed. Alexander Carlyle (London: J. Lane, 1904), 2:51–52. Quoted in Carr, "John Forster," p. 413.

8. *The Letters of Charles Dickens*, Pilgrim Edition, ed. Graham Storey and K. J. Fielding (Oxford: Clarendon Press, 1981), 5:289.

9. Ibid.

10. Ibid., p. 290.

11. "The Life and Adventures of Oliver Goldsmith," *Athenaeum*, 22 April 1848, p. 405.

12. [Thomas De Quincey], "The Life and Adventures of Oliver Goldsmith," *North British Review* 9 (May 1848):187.

13. [Edward Bulwer], *"The Life and Adventures of Oliver Goldsmith. A Biography, in Four Books,"* *Edinburgh Review* 88 (July 1848):221.

14. Ibid., pp. 224, 225

15. "To Charles Dickens," in *The Life and Adventures of Oliver Goldsmith*, n.p.

16. Carr, "John Forster," p. 253.

17. [Fitzgerald], *John Forster*, pp. 9–10.

18. "The Literary Examiner," *Examiner and London Review*, June 5, 1869, p. 356.

19. Edward Dowden. "Walter Savage Landor," *Fortnightly Review*, August 1, 1869, p. 122.

20. [R. Monckton Milnes], *"Walter Savage Landor: A Biography,"* *Edinburgh Review* 130 (July 1869):219.

21. [Eliza Lynn Linton], *"Walter Savage Landor: A Biography,"* *North British Review*, n.s. 11 (July 1869):566–67.

22. *Letters*, 5:289.

23. Davies, "Striving," p. 40.

24. "Literary," *Examiner*, November 16, 1872, p. 1132.

25. Whitwell Elwin, *"The Life of Charles Dickens,"* *Quarterly Review* 132 (January 1872):125, 147.

26. [Fitzgerald], *John Forster*, p. 15.

27. Charles Richard Sanders, "Carlyle's Letters," *Bulletin of the John Rylands Library* 30 (1955):223.

28. *Saturday Review*, November 23, 1872, p. 668.

29. *The Letters of Charles Dickens*, Pilgrim Edition, ed. Madeline House and Graham Storey (Oxford, 1965), 1:xi. See pp. xi–xvii for full discussion of Forster's uses of Dickens's letters.

30. Alec W. Brice, "The Compilation of the Critical Commentary in Forster's *Life of Charles Dickens,*" *Dickensian* 70 (1974):120. Brice offers a full analysis and rationale for Forster's "borrowing" the work of others in his commentary.

31. Davies, "Striving," p. 47.

Chapter Five

1. [Fitzgerald], *John Forster,* pp. 1–2.

2. Quoted in James A. Davies, "Forster and Dickens: The Making of Podsnap,"*Dickensian* 70 (1974):155.

3. Johnston, "John Forster," p. 361.

4. Gardiner, "Mr. John Forster," p. 122.

5. "John Dryden and Jacob Tonson," 1:55.

Selected Bibliography

PRIMARY SOURCES

Note: This section takes only selected examples from Forster's extensive periodical writing. No complete listing of these works is available. For a fuller indication of the range of Forster's publications, see the Chronology.

1. Histories and Historical Biographies

Arrest of the Five Members by Charles the First. London: J. Murray, 1860.

Cabinet Cyclopaedia: Lives of Eminent British Statesmen, edited by Dionysius Lardner. Vols. 2, 3, 4, 6–7. London: Longmans, 1836–1839.

"The Civil Wars and Oliver Cromwell." *Edinburgh Review* 103 (January 1856):1–54.

Debates on the Grand Remonstrance, November and December, 1641. London: J. Murray, 1860.

Historical and Biographical Essays. 2 vols. London: J. Murray, 1858. Vol. 1 is historical and includes a slightly expanded version of "The Civil Wars and Oliver Cromwell."

"A History for Young England." *Jerrold's Shilling Magazine* 1–4 (1845–1846).

Sir John Eliot: A Biography. 2 vols. London: Longmans, 1864.

The Statesmen of the Commonwealth of England. London: Longmans, 1840. Reprints the biographies of the *Cabinet Cyclopaedia* with an introductory "Treatise on the Popular Progress in English History."

2. Literary Biographies

"Charles Churchill." *Edinburgh Review* 81 (January 1845):46–88.

"Daniel De Foe." *Edinburgh Review* 82 (October 1845):480–532.

The Life and Adventures of Oliver Goldsmith. London: Bradbury and Evans, 1848. Revised and expanded for a second edition, *The Life and Times of Oliver Goldsmith.* London: Bradbury & Evans, 1854.

The Life of Charles Dickens. 3 vols. London: Chapman & Hall, 1872–1874.

The Life of Jonathan Swift. Vol. 1. London: J. Murray, 1875.

"Richard Steele." *Quarterly Review* 96 (March 1855):509–68.
"Samuel Foote." *Quarterly Review* 95 (September 1854):483–548.
Walter Savage Landor: A Biography. 2 vols. London: Chapman & Hall, 1869.
Historical and Biographical Essays. Vol. 2. London: J. Murray, 1858. Reprints, in slightly expanded versions, the four biographical sketches from the *Edinburgh* and the *Quarterly*.

SECONDARY SOURCES

1. Books and Parts of Books

Bliss, Trudy, ed. *Jane Welsh Carlyle: A New Selection of Her Letters*. New York: Macmillan, 1950. Delightful glimpses of both Forster and Carlyle by Carlyle's witty and often sardonic wife.

Collins, Philip. "Dickens' Self-Estimate: Some New Evidence." In *Dickens the Craftsman: Strategies of Presentation,* edited by Robert B. Partlow, Jr. Carbondale: Southern Illinois University Press, 1970. Argues that Forster wrote virtually all of the reviews of Dickens's works in the *Examiner,* even after retiring from the paper in 1856, and that these reviews stress Dickens's own views of his accomplishments.

———, ed. *Dickens: The Critical Heritage*. New York: Barnes & Noble, 1971. Reprints selections of Forster's reviews of Dickens's works and includes contemporary criticism of Forster's *Life* of the novelist.

DeVane, William Clyde, and Knickerbocker, Kenneth Leslie, eds. *New Letters of Robert Browning*. New Haven, Conn.: Yale University Press, 1950. Contains in the letters to Forster a clear idea of the value Browning placed on Forster as a personal friend, confidant, and sometime adviser.

Dexter, Walter, ed. *The Letters of Charles Dickens*. 3 vols. London: Nonesuch Press, 1938. With the Pilgrim Edition (House below) the best documentary evidence for the relationship between Dickens and Forster.

Ellis, S. M. *William Harrison Ainsworth and His Friends*. 2 vols. London: John Lane, 1911. Particularly valuable for the relationship between Forster and Ainsworth in the 1830s and 1840s when the two men and Dickens were often an inseparable threesome.

Elwin, Malcolm. "John Forster." In *Victorian Wallflowers*. London: Jonathan Cape, 1934. Excellent survey of Forster's career and the important literary men and women who were his friends.

————. *Landor: A Repleven.* London: Macdonald, 1958. Valuable for the Forster-Landor relationship and for material that Forster suppressed or otherwise altered in his biography of Landor.

Elwin, Whitwell. "John Forster." Introduction to *Catalogue of Printed Books, Forster Collection.* London: H. M. Stationery Office, 1888. A fine, sympathetic portrait of Forster's life and career by the editor of the *Quarterly Review,* a close friend in Forster's later years.

[Fitzgerald, Percy.] *John Forster by One of His Friends.* London: Chapman & Hall, 1903. Appreciative anecdotal descriptions of Forster's personality and activities as seen by a younger writer he befriended and encouraged.

House, Madeline; Tillotson, Kathleen; et al. *The Letters of Charles Dickens.* Pilgrim Edition. Vols. 1–5. Oxford: Clarendon Press, 1965–. With the Nonesuch edition of Dickens's letters (Dexter above), the greatest single documentary source defining the long-standing and fruitful relationship between Forster and the novelist.

Johnson, Edgar. *Charles Dickens: His Tragedy and Triumph.* 2 vols. New York: Simon & Schuster, 1952. With Forster's own *Life,* the best description and assessment of the Dickens-Forster friendship.

Kent, Charles. "John Forster." *Dictionary of National Biography.* Vol. 7. London: Oxford University Press, 1922. Most accessible brief survey of Forster's life, noting the major facts and important dates in his career.

Litzinger, Boyd, and Smalley, Donald, eds. *Browning: The Critical Heritage.* New York: Barnes & Noble, 1970. Reprints selections of Forster's reviews of Browning's works, allowing valuable perspective on Forster's assessments through comparison with other contemporary reviews also reprinted.

Morley, Henry. "Biographical Sketch of Mr. Forster." In *Handbook of the Dyce and Forster Collections in the South Kensington Museum.* London: Chapman & Hall, 1880. With Whitwell Elwin's account (above), the fullest assessment of Forster's life and career written by a contemporary, in this instance by the man who succeeded him as editor of the *Examiner.*

Ray, Gordon N., ed. *The Letters and Private Papers of William Makepeace Thackeray.* 4 vols. Cambridge, Mass.: Harvard University Press, 1945–1946. Excellent source for understanding Thackeray's assessment of Forster during periods of both friendliness and heated debate, for example over the issue of the dignity of literature as a profession.

Renton, Richard. *John Forster and His Friendships.* London: Chapman & Hall, 1912. An appreciative biography of Forster's relationships with important contemporaries. Contains numerous illustrations, but of limited critical interest.

Shannon, Edgar Finley, Jr. *Tennyson and the Reviewers.* New York: Archon Books, 1967. Generous excerpts of Forster's reviews of the poet considered in perspective with other contemporary reviews.

Shattuck, Charles H., ed. *Bulwer and Macready.* Urbana: University of Illinois Press, 1958. Principally through letters provides a detailed account of Forster's involvement in the creation, staging, and reviewing of Bulwer's dramas as acted by Macready.

Tillotson, Geoffrey, and Hawes, Donald, eds. *Thackeray: The Critical Heritage.* London: Routledge & Kegan Paul, 1968. Excerpts selected Forster reviews of Thackeray's works that chart the critic's reserve about some of the novelist's major fiction even as he acknowledges Thackeray's genius.

Toynbee, William, ed. *The Diaries of William Charles Macready 1833–1851.* 2 vols. London: Chapman & Hall, 1912. Gives a wonderfully vital accounting from the perspective of the great actor of Forster as friend, confidant, and not infrequently thorn-in-the-side during the early years of the Bulwer, Browning, Macready, Forster relationships.

2. Articles

Brice, Alec W. "The Compilation of the Critical Commentary in Forster's *Life of Charles Dickens.*" *Dickensian* 70 (1974):185–90. Discusses Forster's inclusion of earlier published criticism of Dickens's works—Forster's own and unlabeled critiques by others—and offers a rationale for such borrowings in the *Life.*

————. "Reviewers of Dickens in the *Examiner:* Fonblanque, Forster, Hunt, and Morley." *Dickens Studies Newsletter* 3 (September 1972):68–80. Argues that, unexpectedly, most of the reviews of Dickens's works in the *Examiner* between 1836 and 1855 were not written by Forster but distributed among four reviewers.

Davies, James A. "Charles Lamb, John Forster, and a Victorian Shakespeare." *Review of English Studies,* n.s. 26 (1975):442–50. Details the personal and literary influence of Charles Lamb on Forster as a critic, particularly in Forster's critical views of Shakespeare and his works when presented upon the stage.

————. "Forster and Dickens: The Making of Podsnap." *Dickensian* 70 (1974):145–58. Delineates the veritable love-hate feelings Dickens manifested toward Forster, to whom he admitted owing so much, particularly highlighting the novelist's hostility in the later years to the moral, upright, eminent Victorian Forster by showing how the obnoxious middle-class boor Podsnap is modeled upon prominent Forster characteristics parodied and caricatured.

————. "Leigh Hunt and John Forster." *Review of English Studies,* n.s. 19 (1968):25–40. Traces the multiple roles Forster played in his thirty-year relationship with Hunt, showing Forster both helping and dominating him. Apparent, too, is Forster's embracing of many of Hunt's critical precepts.

————. "Striving for Honesty: An Approach to Forster's *Life.*" *Dickens Studies Annual* 7 (1978):34–48. Argues that Forster's biography of Dickens is a significant advance in candor even over the *Landor* and that both biographies represent a movement away from the blatant idealization characterizing Forster's portraits of eighteenth-century literary figures.

Fielding, K. J. "Forster: Critic of Fiction." *Dickensian* 70 (1974):159–70. Describes Forster's perspective on fiction as moralistic, idealistic, and optimistic, favoring moderation and opposing sensationalism, and influenced by Shakespeare, Elizabethan drama, and eighteenth-century novelists.

————. "Thackeray and the Dignity of Literature." *TLS,* 19 September 1958, p. 536; 26 September 1958, p. 552. Outlines the "Dignity of Literature" movement and Forster's quarrels with Thackeray over the respect due authors from the public and among themselves because of the importance of their calling.

Fitzgerald, Percy. "John Forster: A Man of Letters of the Old School— A Reminiscence." *Month* 96 (July-December 1900):361–83. Wonderful anecdotes of Forster's personal behavior and manners; an appreciative portrait by a younger writer for whom Forster served as a mentor.

Gardiner, Samuel R. "Mr. John Forster." *Academy* 9 (January-June 1876):122. A generous and appreciative obituary notice assessing Forster as a writer of history by a prominent fellow historian.

Harle, William Lockey. "John Forster: A Sketch." *Monthly Chronicle of North-Country Lore and Legend* 2 (February 1888):49–54. Appreciative biographical survey, particularly of Forster's early days in Newcastle and of his family there.

"History of the *Examiner.*" *Eclectic Magazine* 27 (October 1852):230–34. Describes the substantial prestige of the *Examiner* as a just and accurate critical voice in literature and politics and praises Forster's editorship and his own writing in the paper.

Horne, R. H. "John Forster: His Early Life and Friendships." *Temple Bar* 46 (January-April 1876):491–505. Sometimes amusing anecdotes by one of Forster's fellow journalists and critics who had known him since his early days on the *True Sun,* but the tone and substance offer, on balance, a negative portrait of Forster both as a man and as a writer.

Jerrold, Blanchard. "John Forster." *Gentleman's Magazine,* n.s. 16 (January-June 1876):313–19. Generally unflattering anecdotes about Forster's personality and behavior, including his engagement to "LEL," by the son of Forster's old friend Douglas Jerrold.

Sanders, Charles Richard. "Carlyle's Letters." *Bulletin of the John Rylands Library* 38 (1955):199–224. Traces through Carlyle's letters the fond regard each held for the other and includes many judgments of contemporaries and friends that Carlyle shared with Forster.

Tillotson, Kathleen, and Burgis, Nina. "Forster's Reviews in the *Examiner,* 1840–1841." *Dickensian* 68 (1972):105–8. Focusing exclusively on two years of Forster's reviews, the authors show the range of Forster's interests and demonstrate his role as a "serious and responsible" critic.

Vallance, Rosalind. "Forster's *Goldsmith.*" *Dickensian* 71 (1975):21–29. Assesses Forster's *Goldsmith,* in both editions, particularly focusing upon what in Goldsmith would have attracted Forster and emphasizing Dickens's appreciation of Forster's biography.

Woolley, David. "Forster's *Swift.*" *Dickensian* 70 (1974):191–204. Describes Forster's severe ill health, his manner of writing the *Swift,* its critical reception, and the breadth of Forster's collection of Swiftiana now in the Forster Collection at the Victoria and Albert Museum.

3. Dissertations

Braymer, John Wilbert. "The Literary Biographies of John Forster." Ph.D. diss., University of Tennessee, 1977. Valuable for background on biographical theories in Forster's time and the ways that his biographies do and do not reflect these theories.

Carr, Sister Mary Callista. "John Forster: A Literary Biography to 1856." Ph.D. diss., Yale University, 1956. Excellent discussion of Forster's life and relationships with important contemporaries drawing heavily on his journalism.

Johnston, Elizabeth. "John Forster: Critic." Ph.D. diss., University of Pittsburgh, 1947. Focusing wholly upon Forster's criticism, principally from the *Examiner* in the 1830s and 1840s, examines Forster's critical theories of literature, drama, history, and biography.

Index